R I C H   B

10 *Life-Changing*

ATTITUDES

that will make you a

FINANCIAL

SUCCESS

Published by
ABC Book Publishing

AbcBookPublishing.com
Printed in U.S.A.

10 Life-Changing Attitudes That Will Make You a Financial Success

All scripture quotations, unless otherwise indicated, are taken from the *Holy Bible, New International Version*®. *NIV*®. Copyright © 1973, 1978, 1984 by International Bible Society. Used by permission of Zondervan Publishing House. All rights reserved.

Other Versions used are:

AMP- Amplified Bible.

Amer. Std.-American Standard Version, 1901.

KJV-King James Version. Authorized King James Version.

*NASB-*Scripture taken from the *New American Standard Bible*, ©1960, 1962, 1963, 1968, 1971, 1972, 1973, 1975, 1977 by The Lockman Foundation. Used by permission.

Scripture taken from the *New King James Version*. Copyright © 1979, 1980, 1982 by Thomas Nelson, Inc. Publishers. Used by permission. All rights reserved.

Verses marked (*TLB*) are taken from *The Living Bible* © 1971. Used by permission of Tyndale House Publishers, Inc., Wheaton, IL 60189. All rights reserved.

Scripture taken from *THE MESSAGE: The Bible in Contemporary Language* © 2002 by Eugene H. Peterson. All rights reserved.

This publication is designed to provide interesting reading material and general information with regard to the subject matter covered. It is printed, distributed and sold with the understanding that neither the publisher nor the author is engaged in rendering religious, family, legal, accounting, business, investing, financial, credit, debt or other professional advice. If any such advice is required, the services of a competent professional person should be sought. In summary, the content contained herein is not given as advice, rather it is strictly for the purpose of your reading entertainment.

Every effort has been made to supply complete and accurate information. However, neither the publisher nor the author assumes any responsibility for its use, nor for any infringements of patents or other rights of third parties that would result.

About the Author

Rich Brott holds a Bachelor of Science degree in Business and Economics and a Master of Business Administration.

Rich has served in an executive position with some very successful businesses. He has functioned on the board of directors for churches, businesses, and charities and served on a college advisory board

He has authored over twenty books:

- *5 Simple Keys to Financial Freedom*
- *10 Life-Changing Attitudes That Will Make You a Financial Success*
- *15 Biblical Responsibilities Leading to Financial Wisdom*
- *30 Biblical Principles for Managing Your Money*
- *35 Keys to Financial Independence*
- *A Biblical Perspective On Tithing & Giving*
- *Basic Principles for Maximizing Your Personal Cash Flow*
- *Basic Principles of Conservative Investing*
- *Biblical Principles for Becoming Debt Free*
- *Biblical Principles for Building a Successful Business*
- *Biblical Principles for Financial Success – Student Workbook*
- *Biblical Principles for Financial Success – Teacher Workbook*
- *Biblical Principles for Personal Evangelism (out of print)*
- *Biblical Principles for Releasing Financial Provision*
- *Biblical Principles for Staying Out of Debt*
- *Biblical Principles for Success in Personal Finance*
- *Biblical Principles That Create Success Through Productivity*
- *Business, Occupations, Professions & Vocations in the Bible*
- *Family Finance Handbook*
- *Family Finance Student Workbook*
- *Family Finance Teacher Workbook*
- *Public Relations for the Local Church (out of print)*

He and his wife, Karen, have been married for 35 years. Rich Brott resides in Portland, Oregon, with his wife, three children, son-in-law and granddaughter.

DEDICATION

This book is dedicated to my daughter, Jana Marie. After graduating from Portland Bible College, she then obtained her Bachelor of Science in Molecular Biology from Portland State University. She will soon have a Master of Public Health also from PSU.

Jana has a heart to minister to others, having served for six years in the Legacy Health System. Although we have never discussed it, she already lives these principles; attitudes that will make her a financial success. I am very proud of her accomplishments and ability to be very focused on her goals. She lives her life with excellence.

TABLE OF CONTENTS

INTRODUCTION

a proper attitude and approach to your financial affairs is not only exemplary, but also necessary. In this book you will find 10 life-changing attitudes that will make you a financial success. They are the I Can attitudes. Not only are they life changing, but also very attainable. With the right guidance, you can become debt free. With the proper attitude, you can break bad spending habits. With enough self-discipline, you can pay cash instead of using credit. You can renew your thinking, change your flawed value system, and rise above your burden of debt. If you are financially accountable, you can enjoy life without spending massive amounts of money. If you will let me help you to discover financial solutions and change your improper attitudes, you can change your life!

To a Lifetime of Financial Success!
Rich Brott

Attitude 1

I Can Be Debt Free

C an you be debt free? One person says, "I can," another person says, "I cannot." Which person is correct? Both are correct. If you think you can, most likely you will. It's not so much the power of positive confession or positive thinking, as it is the sheer determination of the human spirit to accomplish what he or she sets out to do.

Being in bondage through debt is sort of the modern-day equivalent to ancient times when a peasant served his lord. Debt is probably one of Satan's best natural weapons. Debt binds so many individuals and families that it is hard to think of a stronger bondage. Debt is the source of strife, heavy burdens and marriage problems. Debt keeps us from being free to fulfill the purposes of God in our lives. Debt also keeps us from giving generously, which can heap enormous blessings upon our lives.

Benjamin Franklin said, "When you run in debt, you give to another power over your liberty." Living within your means is simply not going into debt for any purchase. It means you purchase only things you need, not what you want, and you pay cash for things you need instead of trapping yourself in debt by using credit.

The good news is that everyone can become debt free! By not doing so, you are robbing yourself and robbing your future. Instead of going into debt, would it not be better if the money you pay in interest went into a savings account to help you reach your personal financial goals? By purchasing things now on credit, you are limiting your choices and continuing the unfortunate situation of paying for yesterday's unwise decisions with today's income. You are borrowing from tomorrow to satisfy the whims of today.

It is scriptural to become debt free. Romans 13:7-8 tells us, "Give everyone what you owe him: If you owe taxes, pay taxes; if revenue, then revenue; if respect, then respect; if honor, then honor. Let no debt remain outstanding, except the continuing debt to love one another, for he who loves his fellowman has fulfilled the law."

You can be debt free if you want it badly enough. However long it may take you, it is worth it to begin the journey now. Commit today to become debt free. Don't fill the pockets of the lenders. Instead, fill your own pockets and fund your own dreams.

What is debt? What is a deficit? Do the two words mean the same? We often hear the two used wrongly and completely out of context. In simple terms, we can explain the differences in this way. A deficit is the amount by which a sum of money falls short of the required or expected amount – a shortage.

For example, if you have a monthly spending budget that equals your monthly cash inflow, then you are within budget and have no deficit. However, if your spending exceeds your cash income, then you end with a deficit equal to the amount of the excess spending. The government annual budget deficit is the difference between the amount of money the government spends and the amount it collects.

In the previous example, if you continue deficit spending, the accumulated deficit becomes your debt. This debt, of course, is in addition to all other debt you may have. Debt is an obligation or liability to pay or render something to someone else. It is something owed, such as money, goods, or services. Does debt really matter? Does it affect our lifestyles and us? Why should we be interested in becoming debt free?

Why do people go into debt? Usually it is from ignorance of the eventual financial consequences. True enough, sometimes, unforeseen disasters occur that are completely out of a person's control. This may include the loss of a job or gigantic health and medical bills that come out of nowhere. Usually these are rare exceptions. For most people, debt comes by personal choice: having a personal choice, but making the wrong financial decision.

Some people go into debt because they are not aware of the biblical principles that concern the bondage of debt. Others are fully aware of what the Bible says, but, by their actions, imply they believe these are not commands or requirements, rather suggestions to take or leave. First of all, if Scripture records only suggestions, then is the entire Bible a take-it-or-leave-it opportunity? Second, if it were merely a suggested pattern for living, would you not trust it to be the very best advice you could possibly get?

A lot of denial takes place when it comes to the subject of finances, debt, responsibility and financial accountability. You may deny that debt is bad. You may deny that you really have debt. After all, isn't debt just being past due on your payments? Isn't a loan just a contract? Or you may be thinking, *Sure, I owe some money, but it is manageable and my spending really is not out of control.*

You may say you are young and have plenty of good years to pay off the debt; you can always start reducing your spending tomorrow, or next week, next month or even next year. The problem is that the discipline of tomorrow never comes. I am suggesting that you change your spending behavior right now, today – and make sure that when tomorrow does come, you are well on your way to becoming debt free.

Why should you become debt free? After all, we needed that new car. Our house must have furniture in it. A closet would be useless without a good stock of new shoes and clothes. Of course, we don't have the money now, but we do have credit cards. I am willing to work hard and put in some occasional overtime so that I can put a little extra toward my debt from time to time.

The problem with that kind of thinking is that, every time you attempt to get ahead, you will probably be hit with some other unexpected expense. This is the unintended consequence of debt. Perhaps it is car trouble or an unexpected health-related bill, and because you had neither planned nor budgeted for any unexpected expenses, you seek more credit. This might be another credit card, an extended personal loan or a higher line of credit. At some point though, the deficit spending must stop, the debt must be paid and the savings begun.

TOO MUCH DEBT

Do you have too much debt? How can you tell? Fortunately, potential debt problems can be spotted before they reach the serious stage. By knowing what danger signals to look for, you can take steps to prevent a problem before it occurs.

Go through the checklist below. If any of these danger signals looks familiar, you may be headed for financial trouble.

- You think of credit as cash, not debt.

- Your debts are greater than your assets.

- You owe more than seven creditors.

- You are an impulsive or compulsive shopper.

- You and your spouse are dishonest with each other about your use of credit.

- You don't know how much your monthly living expenses are or the amount of your total debt.

- Your expected increase in income is already committed to paying off debts.

- You depend on extra income, such as earnings by a second person or overtime by the breadwinner, to help you make ends meet.

- You have less than two months' take-home pay in cash or savings where you can get to it quickly.

- You have to pay back several installment payments that will take more than 12 months to pay off.

- You have more than 15 percent of your take-home pay committed to credit payments other than your home mortgage.

- You get behind in utility or rent payments.

- You have to consolidate several loans into one or reduce monthly payments by extending current loans to pay your debts.

- You cannot afford to pay for regular living expenses or credit payments.

- Creditors are sending overdue notices.
- The portion of your income used to pay debts is rising.
- This month's credit balances are larger than last month's.
- You are usually late paying some of your bills.
- You borrow for items you once bought with cash.
- You don't know how much installment debt you owe and you are afraid to add it up.
- You have borrowed money from a new source to pay off an older, perhaps even overdue debt.
- You have borrowed money to pay for regular household expenses such as rent, food, clothing, gas or insurance.
- You have reached your credit limits.
- You hurry to the bank on payday to cover checks already written.
- You no longer can contribute to a savings account or have no savings at all.
- You pay bills with money earmarked for other financial obligations.
- You pay minimum amounts or less on your outstanding debt.
- You use a cash advance from one credit card to make payments on others.
- You've applied for more credit cards to increase borrowing.
- You have drawn from savings to pay regular bills.
- Your liquid assets total less than your short-term debt.

This causes you to....
✓ Take out a loan.
✓ Withdraw savings.

✓ Skip payments.

✓ Pay only the minimum amount due on your charge accounts.

If you identified with two or three of these, it's time to do something about it. If at least four of the above statements applied, examine your budget and look for ways to tighten your belt.

If you identified with five or more, you are probably headed for financial trouble. If you identified with seven or more, then your financial health is in trouble. You are in financial danger!

GETTING INTO DEBT

The road into the misuse of credit is wide, broad, simple, easy, accessible, effortless, uncomplicated, painless, spacious, available and trouble-free.

However there is no quick and easy way out from under a heavy debt load. With debt, you essentially slide in and climb out. Easy to get in, difficult to get out. If you have ever been heavily in debt and burdened down with monthly payments so steep that you could barely keep your head above water and then had to slowly and methodically climb out, then you know that it is an uphill struggle. There is no easy way out. You cannot wave a magic wand and undo in twelve months what it took twelve years to accomplish.

DEBT LIFESTYLE

What about a lifestyle of debt? Is a Christian to borrow? Is debt okay? Some would believe that it is wrong for a Christian to have any debt. Some will say it is alright to borrow for a house, but never to borrow for anything that would depreciate. One of the greatest challenges and hindrances to reaching the world for Christ is this. People who live in a society where there is the possibility of making significant amounts of money all too often spend their way into enormous debt. In doing so, there is little left over (above their tithing) to give to their local church, missions, and evangelism projects. If you have to borrow, learn to give while borrowing.

REPAYING DEBT

It is not wrong to borrow money, but it is wrong to take on debt without the ability to pay it back or with the intention of never repaying what is owed. What is meant in Romans 13:8 when it says not to owe anything to anyone?

> *"Obey the laws, then, for two reasons: first, to keep from being punished, and second, just because you know you should. Pay your taxes too, for these same two reasons. For government workers need to be paid so that they can keep on doing God's work, serving you. Pay everyone whatever he ought to have: pay your taxes and import duties gladly, obey those over you, and give honor and respect to all those to whom it is due. Pay all your debts except the debt of love for others— never finish paying that! For if you love them, you will be obeying all of God's laws, fulfilling all his requirements"* (Romans 13:5-8 *TLB*).

These verses simply mean that you should obey the laws, pay your taxes and repay all of your debts. That just makes good sense. Besides repaying your debts at some future date, you are to pay your creditors on time, with any interest owed. A person who borrows but does not repay is called wicked, meaning wrong, sinful, immoral, evil and depraved.

> *"The wicked borrow and do not repay, but the righteous give generously"* (Psalm 37:21 *NIV*).

THE VALUE OF SELF-CONTROL

If a person or family will live a restrained lifestyle, they will be able to live on thousands of dollars less each year. You should only incur debt when it makes good economic sense. The expense of borrowing should be less than the economic benefit that you will receive.

Don't underestimate God's desire to help you in every way. Over and over the Scriptures indicate that you are to live a controlled and temperate lifestyle.

> *"Now the overseer must be above reproach..... temperate, self-controlled, respectable...."* (I Timothy 3:2 *NIV*).

> *"Thus says the LORD, your Redeemer, the Holy One of Israel: "I am the LORD your God, who teaches you to profit, who leads you by the way you should go"* (Isaiah 48:17 *NKJV*).

Can you become debt free? Yes! Yes, you absolutely can! Why should you desire to become debt free? What should motivate you to stay within a planned budget, pay off debt and keep it paid off? Of course, we could list literally hundreds of reasons, but here are a few to get you started:

➡ 1. **To stay physically healthy.** Debt can cause stress, sickness, depression, illness and poor health. Serious illness can occur when you are stressed out and worn out and your will to fight is diminished. Will you be able to have the money to eat properly or will you and your children be malnourished? How about affording to purchase vitamins, minerals and other health supplements? Can you pay for the proper medicines your physician prescribes for you and your family?

➡ 2. **To stay emotionally healthy.** Long after the pleasure of the purchase is gone, the emotional baggage of repayment goes on and on. If you decide to go ahead and sell the item you were so excited about owning, it is worth a fraction of what you originally paid for it. That is, of course, assuming that someone actually wants to buy it from you and that it has any value at all. Many of your purchases do not. Much debt is brought on by purchases one cannot even recall.

➡ **3. To stay mentally healthy.** Clear thinking and peace of mind cannot be taken for granted. It is hard to have clarity of thought and difficult to make good, logical and well-reasoned financial decisions when you are stressed under a burden of heavy debt.

➡ **4. To maintain a healthy marriage.** Finances are said to be the number one cause of divorce today. This isn't having money or not having money. It has to do with how we handle our money, our discipline, our integrity, our responsibility for it and our account-ability in handling it. Match that with the stress from the weight of debt, along with other communication challenges, and it's a recipe for potential marriage disaster.

➡ **5. To have money for repairs.** If you own or even rent a home, you will need money for repairs and general upkeep. Some examples of possible repairs are a leaky roof, a squeaky furnace, household appliances such as the washer, dryer and refrigerator, and other necessary repairs on vehicles, computers, etc. If you are maxed out on credit card debt and other payments, you won't have the money to pay for unexpected repairs.

➡ **6. To pay for college without adding more debt.** Many kids and adults never have the opportunity to go to college, because of heavy debt loads, even though it is a necessity in today's world. The average American household pays $100 a month in just credit card interest alone. Just think what could happen if that same amount were invested in a stock mutual fund for several years until a child goes off to college. Not only would the child's college tuition be paid for, but there would also be enough money left over to help with other education-related expenses like room and board or textbooks.

➡ 7. **To enjoy life.** Debt has a way of diminishing our quality of life. It often takes the enjoyment out of the simple things in life. After piling up debt after debt, we spend half our lives just paying the cost of interest, in addition to repaying the debt.

➡ 8. **To fulfill dreams.** Debt has a way of dashing our hopes, dimming our vision and destroying our dreams. The more debt we incur, the less chance we have of implementing our goals, executing our ambitions and realizing our dreams.

➡ 9. **To enjoy retirement.** When will you retire? Will it be 15 to 20 years after your friends retire?

Understanding that a lot of choices do come your way and that you have within you the power to improve your financial condition, you will soon understand that you too can be completely debt free. So what is the answer?

Let's start by making sure you know you have too much debt now and need to get out from under the debt burden. In my opinion, any debt is too much debt. To begin your journey out of debt, you must not borrow anymore from this point on. This means saying no to anything but survival needs; i.e., food, water, shelter. Sacrifice all other purchases even though you feel you need them.

Things such as tools, clothes, manicures, hairstylists, movies, eating out, lawn furniture, gifts, going out of town on weekend trips, etc. are definitely out. No more purchases of these kinds. Even some grocery spending should be examined. Specialty foods / drinks and other extras can be trimmed and a great deal of savings can immediately be realized from your food budget.

Of course, you think you have worked hard and deserve some extras, and perhaps you do – but don't! Now is the time to say no and now is the time to give up the extra things you purchase that make you feel good. Will some of this involve saying no to some of your friends? Probably, in the sense that you may not be with them to go shopping, to the beach, to the mountains, to Starbucks, etc.

Just let them know you will be "out of commission" for a while until you get your financial house in order. It is up to you and you alone to decide whether or not your debt is spinning out of control and how you are going to manage it. Cut up the credit cards and get rid of them. Out of sight, out of action and out of mind. This will keep the temptation to spend at a distance.

Though that will stop the bleeding, it does nothing to correct past mistakes. You still have to handle past purchases, past loans and other debt you have incurred. Now that you have stopped the bleeding by saying no to new debt, take all extra cash you have and apply it to old debt. Take any extra money and wipe out all your small debt first. It can be discouraging to limit your wants and not enjoy a few extras as you have in the past, but by doing so, you will soon make some real progress.

As you wipe out smaller debts one by one, you will soon be encouraged and energized to pick up some speed and move ahead to the next debt casualty. Will it be hard work to make these difficult but necessary no-spending choices? Certainly! But keep the bigger picture in mind. Someday you will be debt free and on your way to a better, stress-free life.

Break free from financial bondage. Get the right attitude! Discover that you can be debt free!

Attitude 2

I CAN BREAK BAD SPENDING HABITS

*B*eing in control of your finances means a whole lot more than just earning a greater income, having a better job and controlling your money. It means getting a handle on your bad habits. These might be habits of bad thought, wrong decisions, wrong choices and bad spending habits.

What is it that is motivating you to take on more debt? What is driving your desire to spend until you are out of control? 2 Peter 2:19 mentions this, "For a man is a slave to whatever controls him" (TLB).

How we manage our money affects not only our present, but also our future. It affects how we feel about ourselves and how we react to others. Many of us find ourselves with dismal spending habits that need to be broken. The good news is this: regardless of your past, your future is a clean slate.

Recognizing a problem doesn't always bring a solution, but until we recognize that problem, there can be no solution. Many times the difference between your accomplishment and your failure is your attitude. If you have the attitude that you can take control of your finances and you can break bad habits, then I am confident you will.

You already have all the income you must have to meet your basic needs of food, shelter, and so on. It is amazing how much money we spend on everyday things. Forget all the unnecessary purchases you make, you can save significant dollars just on housing, food, clothing and transportation costs.

Much of a bad spending habit involves seemingly little and simple insignificant purchases. You burn a lot of unaccounted-for cash. Is it a need or is it a want? If it is possible to live life without it, then it's definitely a want. If it is possible to delay the purchase, it's also probably just a want. You must know the difference between a need and a want. Knowledge is good, but your choices must reflect that knowledge. If the potential purchase is a want, then don't buy it. Knowing the difference puts you in control. In the following list, take the test and see if you know the difference.

CHOICE	NEED	WANT
Winter Coat	☐	☐
Larger House	☐	☐
Milk, Bread, & Water	☐	☐
Cable TV	☐	☐
Transportation	☐	☐
Lottery Tickets	☐	☐
Shoes	☐	☐
Designer Jeans	☐	☐
Furnace	☐	☐
New Patio Set	☐	☐
Call Waiting, Voice Mail	☐	☐
Kid's School Supplies	☐	☐
Large Screen TV	☐	☐

Maybe you purchase things just to impress your family, friends and neighbors. Don't worry about keeping up with the Jones'. The only reason you should ever buy something is because you need it, not to impress someone else.

Old bad habits are always hard to break. New good habits are hard to form. The good news is that you CAN break bad spending habits and you CAN get rid of your debt. With the right information, coaching and self-discipline, you CAN move to a much better life of financial stewardship. If you have good financial stewardship in your life, you will be blessed. You see, the result of good stewardship is ongoing and continuous biblical prosperity.

Becoming debt free and honoring God by becoming a person of financial integrity is pleasing to Him. Thus, we may need to begin with a heart transformation and a change in our approach and attitude about managing what He has entrusted to us.

Remember that we own nothing and that we are nothing more than managers of what God has placed in our hands. If we mess up on the little money we have to manage, I cannot imagine God will want to heap more upon us only to see it disappear through bad spending habits, poor purchasing choices and bad financial stewardship.

It is clear that breaking bad spending habits will take some personal discipline. In Proverbs 13:18, we are admonished in this way, "He who ignores discipline comes to poverty and shame, but whoever heeds correction is honored."

Freedom from bad spending takes personal discipline to be sure, not only the discipline of self-restraint, but also the discipline of a good work ethic, careful time management, wise choices and good decisions. Breaking free from poor spending habits takes the personal discipline of knowing where you can go and where you should not go, where you spend your time and the wisdom of how to live below your means.

This means utilizing resources already available to you before jumping into your car, heading for a shopping area and pulling out the credit card to purchase what you perceive you need. This is an example of a bad spending habit you need to break.

Often we form bad financial habits because we are discontent with what we have. Scripture speaks clearly about our bad spending habits when it tell us in Hebrews 13:5, "Keep your lives free from the love of money and be content with what you have".

The end result of continual spending and bad financial habits can eventually lead to bankruptcy. This is something you NEVER want to do. It is dishonest not to repay your debts, and it will also cause financial havoc and personal pain for many years to come. According to Reuters (11/14/2003), bankruptcies are at a record high. Non-business bankruptcies rose 7.8% in fiscal 2003 to 1.63 million. Since 1994, when filings totaled 837,797, bankruptcies in federal court have climbed to an astonishing 98%.

Bad spending habits flourish when we fail to turn down the radio during advertisements, turn off the television during commercials, spend our day off visiting shopping malls, new car dealer lots, etc. Use your free time in productive areas far away from people and places that exist to separate you from your money.

Bad spending habits make you spend hundreds or thousands of dollars without really giving much thought to what you are buying. To stop the process, begin to write down everything you buy for two or three months. Record every nickel, every dime, every cup of coffee and every burger. This simple inconvenient exercise alone will help you to retard your out-of-control spending.

You can break bad spending habits if you will understand all that God has already given to you. If you take the time to appreciate His goodness, you won't always be on the lookout to get something more.

I Timothy 6:6-10 says this:

> *"But godliness with contentment is great gain. For we brought nothing into the world, and we can take nothing out of it. But if we have food and clothing, we will be content with that. People who want to get rich fall into temptation and a trap and into many foolish and harmful desires that plunge men into ruin and destruction. For the love of money is a root of all kinds of evil. Some people, eager for money, have wandered from the faith and pierced themselves with many griefs."*

This verse pretty well puts it all into the proper perspective. We have been given so much already – after all, we came into this world with nothing. If we have food, clothing, shelter, family and friends we have all we need. 2 Corinthians 9:8 lets us know God will always be looking out for you: "And God is able to make all grace abound to you, so that in all things at all times, having all that you need, you will abound in every good work."

Break free from financial bondage. Get the right attitude! Discover how you can break free from bad spending habits!

Attitude 3

I CAN CHOOSE TO PAY CASH

*P*aying cash for a purchase is not generally promoted in our society. In many cases, it is outright discouraged. Why pay cash when you can lease the item? Why pay cash when you can enjoy low-interest financing? Why pay cash when you could be building your personal credit rating? Why pay cash? – you may need it for something else.

Of course, all these statements about not paying cash are just silly. If you buy into this notion that paying cash is bad, you are buying into a lifetime of debt. You are becoming the debtor while someone else is becoming the creditor or lender.

The timeless biblical proverb still remains credible and truthful. According to Proverbs 22:7, "The borrower is servant to the lender." The principle is black and white: there is no room for an alternate interpretation or explanation. You are either a borrower or a lender.

Let's contrast a real-life scenario of the borrower versus the lender that happens tens of thousands of times every day. A person walks into an auto show room and falls in love with that new car or truck that has everything he ever desired.

The design is superb, the model fits his or her personality, the safety features are comforting, the interior is sleek and the instrument panel comes with satellite navigational features. Not to mention the surround sound, satellite radio and the leather interior. Just sitting behind the wheel makes you feel rich and successful and gives you a sense of well being.

Of course, in reality, if you do not have the cash to pay for it, and you are not already completely debt free, you are headed for financial disaster. At the very least, you are falling for a lifestyle of debt that has been disastrous to many people today. Current marketing culture paints a glorious picture of the rich and famous as opposed to the down and out. Yet millions have bought into the payment-poor, debt-bondage lifestyle.

There is a great danger in our society of getting trapped by debt. This chapter will address a number of borrowing and credit issues. Perhaps the greatest need in families today is to understand the consequences of being trapped by debt, with limited income, creating a financial position where recovery seems impossible.

Anyone can find a wealth of information which deals with borrowing, easy credit and debt issues, but the problem counselors often encounter is failing to get people to recognize the seriousness of their actions before they make wrong decisions. All too often, people only want help after their situation has become nearly hopeless. Just know that borrowing can be very hazardous to your financial health and possibly to your mental health, spiritual health and the health of your relationships.

SAY NO TO BORROWING

Too often, people are quick to borrow instead of trusting the Lord to meet their needs. After all, doesn't Scripture tell us that our God is a providing God, and that He will take care of us by meeting our needs? What if we turn to credit and take on new debt, when all along God wanted to show Himself strong on our behalf? Before you run to the bank for a loan, before you pull out the charge card, before you rush to meet your own needs, give time for the provision of God to work.

> *"Not that I am looking for a gift, but I am looking for what may be credited to your account. I have received full payment and even more; I am amply supplied, now that I have received from Epaphroditus the gifts you sent. They are a fragrant offering, an acceptable sacrifice, pleasing to God. And*

my God will meet all your needs according to His glorious riches in Christ Jesus" (Philippians 4:17-19 *NIV*).

We have been taught from childhood to make decisions and move quickly and decisively, so we feel compelled to hurry to fix our own problems. Yet, in spite of this need for speed, we should be patient in waiting on God. We should be cautious about always making our own way independently instead of seeking the wisdom of God.

> *"Let the wicked forsake his way and the evil man his thoughts. Let him turn to the LORD, and He will have mercy on him, and to our God, for He will freely pardon. 'For My thoughts are not your thoughts, neither are your ways My ways,' declares the LORD. 'As the heavens are higher than the earth, so are My ways higher than your ways and my thoughts than your thoughts'"* (Isaiah 55:7-9 *NIV*).

EASY CREDIT IS NOT SO EASY!

The problem with easy credit is that there are always banking institutions willing to give you more money than you have the ability to repay. If you need to borrow a thousand dollars for an unexpected need because you have not set aside dollars for that purpose, the lending institutions will try to give you several thousand more than you actually need. While at first blush that may give you great pride and confidence, thinking that someone really believes in you, in reality, the only way a bank makes money is to lend it out.

If you receive seven or eight thousand dollars and you only needed one thousand, rest assured—you will find a way to spend the extra. It will disappear before you know where it went. The less you borrow, the less you pay back and the more you have available to give to missions and the needs of others. Credit should always be the exception and not the rule.

One of the problems with obtaining credit is that you are presuming that nothing is going to change for the worse in the future. You are assuming you and your spouse will have adequate income for repayment, that your jobs are secure and that your income stream will be the same or more in later years.

There is a danger in making assumptions. It could be that your intended source of repayment changes. Jobs are lost; the value of stocks and bonds can decline or even disappear; assets may not appreciate as quickly as anticipated or may even lose their value.

> *"Now listen, you who say, 'Today or tomorrow we will go to this or that city, spend a year there, carry on business and make money.' Why, you do not even know what will happen tomorrow. What is your life? You are a mist that appears for a little while and then vanishes. Instead, you ought to say, 'If it is the Lord's will, we will live and do this or that'"* (James 4:13-15 *NIV*).

A SLAVE TO DEBT

A person who is deep in debt feels like they are in bondage. They are so burdened down with the heavy load of debt, it is like becoming a servant to your creditors. You work all day for days on end just to meet your payment obligations to your debtors. You gladly volunteer for all the overtime you can get and work a part-time job in the evenings or on weekends, all for the purpose of getting a larger paycheck so you can turn it over to someone else. Well, all of this is not breaking news. You knew about it long before you borrowed the money. You read about it in Scripture.

> *"The rich rule over the poor, and the borrower is servant to the lender"* (Proverbs 22:7 *NIV*).

Look at the difference between the borrower and the lender in purchasing just one moderately priced vehicle. Given a very common loan repayment schedule of six years, a huge gap occurs between the two situations. Here are the two choices: 1) making vehicle loan payments 2) taking that very same payment and investing it in the equity market yielding average equity returns over the past 40 years.

The real difference is this. The borrower makes the same payment the lender (investor) does for the exact same time period. When the time period is up, the borrower stops making all payments; so does the investor.

At the end of the six years, the borrower has a used vehicle of questionable value. At the end of six years, the person who chooses not to borrow for a new car or truck, but instead invests the exact same payment, has a total sum of $55,741. This is just for the onetime purchase of just one vehicle.

Wait, that's not all. Both persons have made the very same monthly payment. However, the investor (the one who does not borrow) makes no more payments, but continues to let the accumulation of his or her six-year payments grow in the marketplace, gaining return upon compound return at the very same rate.

In just 4 additional years, the lump sum of payments has now turned into $90,082. Add on another 10 years and it becomes $299,081; yet another 10 years and the total is now $992,985. Finally, after another 10 years it has grown to $3,296,826.

Amazing! All the accumulation has come from just six years of monthly payments. The borrower described in Proverbs 22:7 has a used vehicle of questionable value after six years. But with absolutely no additional contributions, look what the wise person of Proverbs 22:7 has accumulated! This is a clear reminder that the Bible really does make a lot of sense.

It's Your Choice	Your Total Cost	Value in 6 years	Value in 10 years	Value in 20 years	Value in 30 years	Value in 40 years	Total Loss/ Gain
Auto Loan	$37,872	$5,000	$1	$0	$0	$0	($37,871)
Invest instead	$37,872	$55,741	$90,082	$299,081	$992,985	$3,296,826	$3,258,954

Here are the details for your review:

VEHICLE LOAN

Cost of Vehicle:	$30,000	
Interest Rate:	8%	
Number of Monthly Payments:	72	
Monthly Payment:		$526
Total of Payments:		$37,872
Year 6 Vehicle Value:		$5,000
Total Loss on Payments:		($32,872)
Year 10 Vehicle Value:		$1
Total Loss of Payments:		($37,871)

INVEST INSTEAD

Interest Rate:	12%	
Number of Monthly Payments:	72	
Monthly Payment:	$526	
Total of Payments:	$37,872	
Year 6 Investment Value:		$55,741
Total Gain on Payments:		$17,869
Year 10 Investment Value:		$90,082
Total Gain on Payments:		$52,210
Year 20 Investment Value:		$299,081
Total Gain on Payments:		$261,209

Year 30 Investment Value:	$992,985
Total Gain on Payments:	$955,113
Year 40 Investment Value:	$3,296,826
Total Gain on Payments:	$3,258,954

Why are you encouraged to use credit instead of paying with cash? Two reasons are clear to me.

1. If you pay cash, you are likely to be more careful in your purchase.

a. You may not make the purchase at all.

b. You may delay the purchase until you have enough cash.

c. You may decide there are other priorities for you cash.

d. You may press the vendor for a better deal.

e. If you do not get a substantial discount on the potential purchase you may just walk away.

2. If you pay cash, the dealer, the vendor, the store, etc., will not get more benefit from your purchase by gaining from a financing deal.

a. Carrying your financing increases the value of your purchase.

b. Carrying your financing provides ongoing interest income.

c. Offering you credit helps push you toward a purchase.

d. Offering you credit helps you make a quick decision.

e. Offering "easy credit terms" gets more types of people in the door to make a purchase.

f. Offering to finance the deal gets you into the store or showroom much quicker.

g. Offering to loan you the money makes you think about a purchase you would not have previously considered.

You need to know that vendors who are offering you easy financing for your purchase don't do so for YOUR benefit. It is not offered to you because you are so well liked that the store or dealer just wants to make your life a bit easier. Offering to finance your purchase is purely in the self-interest of the vendor.

Many people, even so-called consultants, will tell you that there is "good debt" and "bad debt." Wrong! Please don't buy into the "good debt" / "bad debt" discourse. ALL debt is bad! Yes, at times we are swayed into a purchase because we don't have the cash, but that does not make the debt good!

The only debt that even comes close to making some short-term sense is a home mortgage. If you cannot make the payments on a 15-year mortgage however, you are probably buying too much house. My recommendation is to limit your home mortgage to 15 years and then do everything in your power to shorten that debt period by making extra payments toward your principle balance.

WHY IS DEBT DANGEROUS?

Americans are literally trillions of dollars in debt. That is the danger of credit, which is simply the ability to borrow money. In short, it is the spending of money today that will be tomorrow's income. Most economists would say that credit is an important part of the ability of individuals, families, cities and ultimately nations to function in a financial world. Credit consists of unpaid balances on auto loans, credit cards, student loans and generally any non-mortgage debt.

One of the real dangers of excessive borrowing is that it creates high monthly payments, which often strain even well-planned budgets. The pace of borrowing often exceeds the family's growth in income and leads to a form of credit-debt bondage. The interest expense of credit debt is often very high. Banks and other lending institutions often will loan to people with a higher credit risk, but do so at the expense of the borrower.

This is a huge profit opportunity for the company. Often those that do not qualify for the terms of a regular loan still get money, but at an interest rate several points higher than normal. Of course, most individuals, families and businesses will quickly agree to this because, in reality, they need the money at any cost.

People that have high monthly credit payments often sacrifice their other financial goals just to make their payments. This is a very serious offense. By not investing in a house, savings account or other forms of investment, they seriously put their future retirement in question.

Excessive debt cannot be ignored. It will not go away. You can ignore past-due bills, but you do so at the risk of finding yourself in even worse circumstances. A chain of events is triggered when you do not pay your bills. Creditors can take action against you, the past-due bills can be turned over to a debt collector, your property can be repossessed and your wages garnished.

While debt bondage is the result of unwise decisions and excess credit purchases, there is no easy way out. The reason why people find themselves in this position is because they spend more than they earn and the only way out is to spend less and pay the difference on their debt balance. The only way out of this dangerous situation is to get control of your spending and put yourself on a budget, which we defined earlier as a written plan that provides oversight and guidance to your spending habits.

IF YOU MUST, BORROW LESS

It is always wise to borrow less rather than more. Cultivate the mind-set that you will only borrow for absolute necessities and that you will repay the loan at the earliest possible date. Paying back a larger amount than the required fixed payment will help you retire the debt early. What should you not be getting a loan for and what would be something worth borrowing for? In general, it all depends on your ability to repay the loan within a practical period of time.

While you could obtain credit to purchase an asset with reasonable potential to gain in value, you should not borrow for something that will continue to lose its value from the moment you buy it. Another sensible cause for which to borrow money would be for something obtained that would bring you income opportunity. If you have a skill or a trade and purchasing a particular tool or machine would generate additional income for you, then credit might be a possibility to explore.

Shun Indulgence

Don't get in the habit of buying something before you need it or because you think you might use it at some future date. Indulgence because you feel that you owe it to yourself or it will help your self-esteem is a very bad habit to get into.

You can develop habits that will insure financial success, regardless of how much or how little your income is. Many make very little over a lifetime, yet manage to save enough for a debt free and secure retirement.

No Credit Card Debt

Your current credit card debt represents more than just the fact that you owe money. It represents the fact that you are spending more money than you are making. It represents the fact that, depending on how much you owe, you could be out of touch with your financial situation. It represents the fact that you need to attend to paying it off now—or it will likely get worse before it gets better.

If you are going to have a credit card, pay it off in full at the time of each statement. If you cannot do that, you have no business carrying a card with you. Pay cash instead.

Live Within Your Means

Scripture says that the poor will always be with us, but it does not say that none of them will be Christians. If you've ever wondered, "I cannot understand why God has not made me rich yet," we have no magic formulas but this one. Live within, not above, your income!

A friend of mine had purchased a couple of fine houses, but then sold them to pay off debts, only to get into debt all over again.

Cultivate the mindset that you will only borrow for absolute necessities.

Please understand this. You will never win the lottery, so quit spending money on tickets. Quit spending money as if you were about to win the lottery. God's ways are not about windfall income like the lottery. His ways are about thriftiness, staying out of debt, working hard and serving Him. How does one get out of debt? Exactly the same way it was accumulated....one step at a time.

If you give a man a fish, you can feed him for a day. If you teach him to fish, you can feed him for life. The real help comes in changed attitudes that cause you to move from a lifestyle of debt to the freedom of being debt-free and becoming financially independent.

Some go into debt for so-called investment purposes. They are buying second homes, seaside properties, even speculating in commercial development or in the house rental market. This is a volatile place to put your personal finances. Unless you have substantial cash available to cover for an enormous potential loss in income, run away from such so-called investing.

Coming from the corporate world, I can tell you of faulty thinking firsthand. During the boom and subsequent bust of the 90s, a common practice was to make large purchases via leasing contracts. Virtually everything was leased. Fleets of trucks, manufacturing equipment, buildings, and so on were all leased instead of purchased outright.

This produced a couple of scenarios. First, it encouraged buying even when no cash was available. Second, it kept the "corporate debt" off the Statement of Financial Condition, commonly called the balance sheet. Third, many assets owned outright by the company were sold for cash and then leased back from the new owner. This supposedly freed up corporate cash for other things.

I saw great companies with substantial real estate and other corporate assets proceed to sell off the assets, receive the cash, and then watch the cash simply disappear over a short time period. The company was left with long-term leasing debt and a huge burden to bear for many years to come.

The bottom line of the leasing scandals I witnessed was that the greedy corporate executives boosted the value of their corporate parachutes, and boosted the value of their personal stock options. They received unprecedented amounts of company bonuses because of their wonderful achievement of improving the corporate financial condition. After many great personal bonuses and benefits, the executives would move on to other companies and new opportunities to do the same all over again.

The real sadness of going into corporate debt was that the investors never knew what was happening to the companies in which they had invested their lifesavings. The leasing debt was never a part of the corporate balance sheet and because of loopholes in the law, the company auditors never disclosed the debt in the financial reports.

If corporate debt is good, than why is one of the most successful companies ever to grace planet Earth completely debt free? If debt is so good and provides so much so-called tax relief, why is the company that produced the richest man in the world debt free? Of course, I am talking about Microsoft, which has no debt and more than fifty billion in cash! That's a cool fifty-thousand-million dollars. Not only this company, but also many others are debt free.

Thousands of others like it have chosen to have absolutely no corporate debt. These companies include Walgreen, Cisco Systems and William Wrigley. Cisco Systems has never borrowed money and does not plan to. Cisco Systems, the networking company, funds its own expansion instead of borrowing money.

Not having debt helped companies survive during the dot-com bust. As I am writing this, Cisco earned $772 million during its most recent quarter, while Lucent (a company in great debt) lost $7.9 billion. Lucent pays interest each quarter on $3.2 billion. Walgreen expands its drugstores by the monthly cash it generates. Its corporate philosophy, according to a company representative, is "We're a pay-as-you-go type." A competitor of Walgreen is Rite Aid, which struggles with paying interest on a heavy debt load of $3.7 billion.

Wrigley, the chewing-gum maker, has never had any long-term debt since it was founded some 110 years ago. Ross Stores doesn't borrow any money to expand. Each new store costs $1.3 million to open, but generates an average of $6 million in revenue the first year of business. In the Northwest USA where I live, 34 major companies alone have no debt.

Use the information I have just provided to think about paying cash. If you don't have the cash, don't make the purchase! Use the "cash paying" model of these companies to improve your own personal family financial balance sheet. Perhaps you have made some mistakes in the past. Yes, you must now dig yourself out of debt. Your past is important, but not nearly as important to your present as the way you see your future.

So is there really good debt? Not in my opinion. Perhaps, at best, some debt is tolerable for a short time period if you need a roof over your head or a yard for the kids to enjoy. Make a commitment to your future and the future opportunity of your family. Choose now to pay cash.

Break free from financial bondage. Get the right attitude! Discover how you can choose to pay cash!

Attitude 4

I Can Renew My Thinking

Do you suffer the consequences of bad financial decisions because you have faulty thinking? Do you need to renew your thinking? Life seems busy as we hurry through our hours, days, weeks, months and years. At various seasons of our lives we need to stop and re-assess what we have been doing, where we are now and the direction we are headed.

Proverbs 14:12

> *"There is a way that seems right to a man, but in the end it leads to death."*

Proverbs 3:5

> *"Trust in the LORD with all your heart and lean not on your own understanding."*

Proverbs 3:7

> *"Do not be wise in your own eyes; fear the LORD and shun evil."*

What past financial decisions have you made that affect the way you are now living? Many of those in financial difficulty really don't know how they got into trouble. They just know that all of a sudden they found themselves in financial jeopardy.

It is easy to let our decision making be based upon our current surroundings and the circumstances in which we find ourselves. Is your financial future being influenced by your season in life, your current friends and your need to be accepted? If so, this influence can be positive and productive if you have the right influences, or it can be negative and devastating if you are keeping the wrong company.

Our culture often pushes greed, materialism and a mind-set of "you've got to have it all right now." Our judgment and decision making are easily influenced by the commercials we see and hear, by the friendships we keep and by are inability to distinguish our needs from our wants.

Proverbs 23:4 says, *"Do not wear yourself out to get rich; have the wisdom to show restraint."* We need to be on guard against personal greed that will lead us to want everything we see and cause us to spend all our energies in a futile attempt to have it all. We must restrain ourselves from seeking things even when we have enough money to purchase them. Additionally, we should also restrain ourselves from purchases for which we have no money and have to go into debt to obtain them.

Going into debt for wants certainly suggests that a person needs a renewal of the mind and a change in the thinking process. Debt is potentially enslaving and we should avoid it at all costs. Proverbs 22:7 makes this very clear to us when it says, *"The rich rule over the poor, and the borrower is servant to the lender."*

Whether we want to admit it or not, we are influenced by the common thinking prevalent in our "get it now" society. Every once in a while, even normally rational people have to step back and review how we are affected by our surroundings.

Do you have a faulty system of input and thinking? Are you influenced by others to make bad financial decisions? We may find that we need to "renew our thinking." In Romans 12:2, the apostle Paul says we are not to conform or go along with the thinking that is prevalent in our world, but we should think differently, or be transformed.

He tells us that this is accomplished by renewing our mind; i.e., our patterns of evaluation, our outlook, our wisdom on any matter, our thoughts, our assessment, our thinking, etc.

Romans 12:2 says, *"Do not conform any longer to the pattern of this world, but be transformed by the renewing of your mind."* The word "transformation" is translated from the same Greek word that also gives us the word "metamorphosis." This word means to change. If we are not to have the same materialistic mind-set that is prevalent in our culture and society today, then we must change our thinking. The changing of our attitudes about matters of personal finance will not come without a renewal of our thinking.

Instead of buying things that you do not need, why not consider investing in someone besides yourself?

Let me give you a possible scenario for buying personal happiness. What if your total income was $50,000 per year. And let's agree that you are by now a faithful and obedient tithe payer; i.e. you give God 10% of your increase and you have become a good steward of the 90% God has entrusted you with. Obviously if you are a good manager you are already living comfortably below the 90% remainder. Now let's suppose that you work for someone else and you receive a $5,000 raise in your annual income. What should you do with that? Should you buy a newer car? How about take a longer vacation. Maybe you could buy more "stuff" so that you need a bigger garage or a larger shed to store it in.

Consider the "happiness" alternative. Instead of using the money to heap new "stuff" upon yourself, why not use the additional increase to help others? Here's a few ideas for you.

$ 5,000 Increase in Personal Income
<$ 500>   additional tithe to your local church
<$1,200>   support a missionary for $100 per month
<$ 500>   support a homeless shelter
<$ 300>   pay some utility bills of an unemployed person
<$ 500>   donate to a food program for the needy
<$ 500>   arrange for a poor family to enjoy a nice Christmas

<$1,000> help a college student with tuition and/or books
<$ 400> buy new tires for an older person on a fixed income
<$ 100> give to a neighbor child to help with summer camp
$ 0   Balance of Increase

Try this one time with your increase and just see whether or not you receive more joy and happiness then you've ever experienced before. Honor the Lord with your increase; honor the Lord with your wealth.

PRAYERS FOR RENEWED THINKING

Do you make time to pray the truths of God's Word over your finances? Nehemiah was a man who understood the power of combining specific prayer with the practical details of his life.

When he first received the report that the walls of Jerusalem had been torn down and destroyed by fire, his first reaction was to turn to God in prayer and fasting (Neh. 1:3-4). When he was later asked by the king about what he would need to rebuild the walls, we read that he first offered up a prayer to God and then asked the king for the specific materials he would need (Neh. 2: 4, 7-8).

Then, when facing heavy opposition during the building project, we read that he responded in two ways. After first crying out to God in prayer (Neh. 4:4, 9), he then placed guards behind the lowest parts of the wall in the most vulnerable places (Neh. 4:13). Nehemiah's mentality for moving forward in his God-given project combined prayer with the practical.

God's Word contains powerful truths which relate to different areas of your finances, including savings, borrowing, investing, and budgeting. We have described some of these practical areas of life with corresponding truths from the Word of God.

Many today have a deep desire to apply the truths of God's Word into our lives. Even if we don't have a huge project in front of us, as Nehemiah did, we have a longing to walk in financial success, wisdom, and freedom.

Desiring financial breakthrough, however, is often a far-cry from reality. When Monday morning rolls around, the kids are still asking for new clothes, the car needs to be fixed, and the bills need to be paid. Imagine that your current financial situation is like a wall that is being built.

Remember that, in Nehemiah's situation, he placed guards behind the most vulnerable places in order to ward off the attacks of the enemy. Do you see any weak, vulnerable areas in your "financial wall" that are prone to attack? How can you make sure that you are moving forward in your financial vision, protected from everyday hindrances? We believe that you need a "Nehemiah mentality" that combines specific prayer with the everyday details of your life.

The financial prayer guide below is intended to help you pray over 14 specific areas of your finances. While some prayer guides are intended to be prayed in full each day, we would suggest a more simple approach for this one, offering up a prayer for your finances in the morning and in the evening. It is our hope that, through adopting a Nehemiah mentality, you can move forward in the financial vision that God has for you!

WEEKLY FINANCIAL PRAYER GUIDE

SUNDAY

Giving
Lord, I thank you for giving the ultimate Gift to me, your Son (John 3:16). *Please help me today to be conscious of giving opportunities* (II Cor. 8:12-15, Col. 4:3-5), *obedient in my tithing* (Mal. 3:10), *and compassionate for those who are in need* (Prov. 19:17).

Wise Decisions
Lord, you are so faithful to give wisdom to me when I ask you for it (James 1:5)! *In my decision-making this week, I ask you for the courage to step out* (Josh. 1:9), *the discernment to weigh the costs involved* (II Cor.

9:7, Lk. 14:28), and the commitment to finish what I have started (Col. 4:17, II Cor. 8:11).

MONDAY

Seeking the Kingdom

Lord, today I acknowledge your command to seek first your kingdom and your righteousness (Matt. 6:33). Help me to avoid the lust for greed and money (I Tim. 6:6-11), to be content with what I have (Heb. 13:5), and to live for eternal things (Phil. 3:19-20).

Sowing

Lord, thank you that you have called me to sow cheerfully and generously, expecting a harvest in time (II Cor. 9:6-15). Help me not to grow weary in well-doing (Gal. 6:9), sowing to please the Spirit (Gal. 6:8) with my words (Eph. 4:29), with my time (I Chron. 12:32), and with my money (II Cor. 9:6-15).

TUESDAY

Stewardship

Lord, I am amazed that you have entrusted me with talents and resources that you want me to multiply (Matt. 25:14-30)! I ask you today for help in being diligent with my time (Ps. 90:12), faithful with my responsibilities (Col. 3:23), and both wise and gracious in my communication with others (Col. 4:6, Prov. 22:11).

Self-discipline

Lord, I need your help to be self-disciplined so that, like an athlete in training, I can win the prize (I Cor. 9:24-27)! Help me to know the short-term and long-term financial goals I need to work on (Col. 1:9-10, Phil. 3:13-14). Please grant me the grace to both resist distractions (Prov. 4:25-26, Ecc. 10:16-17) and take time for creative rest (Ps. 23:2-3).

WEDNESDAY

Persevering

I thank you, Jesus, that when troubles come my way, it is an opportunity for joy (James 1:2)! *In any financial challenges I am facing, I ask you for help to discern the root of the problems* (I Tim. 6:10) *while praising you in the midst of them* (Job 1:21-22, Ps. 27:5-6). *Though life is busy, help me to invest in focused prayers* (Phil. 4:6) *that will give birth to peace* (Phil. 4:7), *new direction* (Acts 13:2-3), *and eventual solutions* (II Chron. 20:13-24).

Vision

I give you praise, Lord, that you've called me to reach forward unto those things that are before me (Phil. 3:13-14). *Grant me great wisdom to lay hold of renewed financial vision for my life* (Col. 1:9-10, Neh. 1:4, 2:4-8), *resisting the procrastination* (Prov. 6:6-11) *and distractions* (Gal. 5:7-9) *that would stand in my way.*

THURSDAY

Planning

Lord, thank you that, by the hand of your Spirit, I am able to make wise plans in how to invest my money, time, and resources (Matt. 25:14-30, I Chron 29:3-5 Zech. 4:6). *Help me to be wise in my budgeting and to close the doors on unnecessary spending* (Prov. 21:20). *Enable me to set aside the time to seek out good counsel* (Prov. 15:22), *making plans that are wise, just, and ordered of You* (Prov. 12:5, Jms. 4:15-16).

Savings

Thanks, Lord, for the simple example of the ants who know how to wisely store up for the future (Prov. 6:8). *Help me not to spend everything I make* (Prov. 21:20), *but to wisely discern the amount I need to set aside for future needs, emergencies, commitments, and long-range goals* (II Cor. 8:10-11, Prov. 6:8, 31:21, 27).

FRIDAY

Debt-free

Lord, your ways are higher (Is. 55:8-9)! *I ask you to renew my mind with your divine perspective about debt, credit, and borrowing* (Prov. 11:15, 22:7, Rom. 13:6-8). *Help me to be intentional about paying off my debts* (Rom. 13:6-8), *and let me be faithful in the little things of life so that you can entrust me with more* (Lk. 16:10-12, 19:18-19).

Wise Lifestyle

Thank you, Lord, that you have called me to be a person who is careful and wise (Eph. 5:15). *In the way that I live, help me to be resourceful and yet generous* (Prov. 21:20, Prov. 11:25), *led by your Spirit in both the little choices I make and in my major decisions* (Lk. 16:10-12, Jms. 4:15). *Let me be known as a person who is full of the Spirit and wisdom* (Acts 6:3).

SATURDAY

Watchman

Lord, you have called me to diligently guard the vulnerable areas of my life that are prone to attack (Prov. 4:20-27, Neh. 4:13, I Pet. 3:11). *Help me to avoid get-rich schemes* (I Tim. 6:9), *unwise investments* (Lk 14:28-30), *hasty purchases* (Prov. 14:8), *and any deceptions of others* (Prov. 9:13-18) *that would cause me to stumble and fall. Make me a diligent watchman* (Neh. 4:13, Ezek. 22:30) *who knows the enemy's schemes in advance* (II Cor. 2:11, II Kgs. 6:10), *guarding and protecting that which you've entrusted to me.*

Investing

Lord, thank you that you've called me to live a life of multiplication and not mere addition (Matt. 13:23, 25:14-30). *As I look to you for vision for the future, help me to consider my options for investing* (Prov. 21:5, 31:16-24), *discerning the proper times* (Ps. 90:12, I Chron. 12:32, Ecc. 8:5-6) *and sowing with wisdom* (Lk 19:13-26).

Break free from financial bondage. Get the right attitude! Discover how you can renew your thinking!

Attitude 5

I Can Change My Flawed Value System

*H*ave the priorities in your financial life been influenced by a faulty system of values? Is your spending out of control because principles of integrity are out of alignment in your life?

A key indicator of strength of character is a person's system of values. Values help each of us determine what is important in our lives. Values set our parameters and provide us with directional guideposts. Our core values and set principles help us make our decisions, and determine our responses to what life hands us. Our actions come from our value system.

A value is a mission, a belief and a set of principles upon which to live our lives. Whether or not they are clearly defined or written upon some paper or e-file, we all live our lives based on some set of personal rules and values. Very few notable people have achieved great accomplishments, enjoyed enormous success or distinguished careers without implementing personal values and underpinning their daily lives with certain principles.

What do you value in life? Are having things more important to you than becoming debt free? Is your work more important to you than your family? Are business contacts more important to you than your friends? Is climbing the corporate ladder of success more important to you than enjoying life itself?

Of course we are not talking about a lack of motivation, laziness or failing to work diligently for our employers, but we are referring to the values we hold close and getting our priorities right. Having a good value system does not come without a monetary cost.

Is accumulating vast resources of money so you can live on Easy Street for the rest of your life part of your value system? Is driving the latest car so you can impress your neighbors and friends part of your value system? Does a sense of pride drive you to continuously out-do others? Are you driven to do more, have more, buy more and show more?

In Luke 12:15 Jesus says, "Watch out! Be on your guard against all kinds of greed; a man's life does not consist in the abundance of his possessions."

A sense of self-worth and all the things that are important in life is directly connected to the core values a person possesses. If you are to be at peace with yourself, your family and your God, you need to rest upon an established base of good personal values, and those values need to drive your every thought, action and reaction. Anything less than that will lead to a violation of the real you. This will lead to confusion, discouragement, frustration and depression.

What are some good core values? What do you value in life? Some important values to consider are as follows:

- financial responsibility
- loyalty
- self-respect
- concern for others less fortunate
- adventure
- effectiveness
- decisiveness
- respect for others
- friendships
- security
- affection
- close relationships
- love
- family
- humor

- justice
- independence
- honesty
- good health
- purity
- spirituality
- reputation
- responsibility
- stability
- hard work
- self-reliance
- selflessness
- accuracy
- excellence
- personal growth

- creativity
- freedom
- diligence
- fairness
- accountability
- orderliness
- accomplishment
- achievement
- truth
- wisdom
- nature
- helping others
- positive attitude
- teamwork
- doing God's work
- trust for others
- inner peace
- emotional well-being
- knowledge
- meaning in life
- faith
- service to others
- resourcefulness
- tradition
- gratitude
- simplicity
- and so on

An important personal value that has nothing to do with money, possessions or things is personal integrity. When you lose your personal integrity you have lost one of the great personal values available to every person alike. This value comes at no economic cost. Compromising integrity for social, economic or financial gain is the fast track to an unhappy life.

Another important personal value that has no economic cost to you is to leave your world (globally and locally) a better place for someone else. Whether you leave a room organized and clean for the next person, a project completed competently, a system working efficiently or a life lived righteously as a model for your children and grandchildren, leave something for someone else.

George Bernard Shaw said, "Life is no 'brief candle' to me. It is a sort of splendid torch which I have got a hold of for the moment, and I want to make it burn as brightly as possible before handing it on to future generations."

Sometimes we find ourselves in conflict with our chosen core values. If you say you value charity, but rarely give of yourself, your time or your money, you are in conflict with your core values and not living your life to its fullest. If you say you value family life, but never spend any time at home, a conflict is occurring in your life. If you say that you value good health, but you have poor eating habits and you never exercise, another conflict is in progress.

I began with the following two questions. Have the priorities in your financial life been influenced by a faulty system of values? Is your spending out of control because principles of integrity are out of alignment in your life?

If you have found that your desires and ambitions have centered on accumulating more and more possessions and keeping ahead of your neighbors, then you have been making financial decisions based upon a defective system of values. Cracks have formed in your foundation. The good news is that those cracks can be repaired.

Financially responsible people who discover that improvements in their value system are needed, make changes and seek changes in the following ways:

➤ Saying, "I'll do it."

➤ Finding an answer for every problem.

➤ By accepting, "I can change."

➤ Looking for a way to make it happen.

➤ Acknowledging, "Why not!"

➤ Saying, "It may be difficult, but it's possible."

➤ By determining, "I can do all things through Christ who strengthens me" (Philippians 4:13).

You can change your faulty financial value system. Instead of valuing things, you can value life. Instead of desiring the latest, the greatest, the best and the rest, you can change yourself and change your life. You can do it with just a bit of encouragement and support. You really CAN rescue your life and liberate your future!

Break free from financial bondage. Get the right attitude! Discover how you can change your flawed value system!

Attitude 6

I Can Rise Above My Burden of Debt

*D*ebt is a burden, a weight, a concern, a worry, and comes with a certain amount of uneasiness. The burden of coping with a large amount of debt is strenuous. Coping with debt-related problems is no picnic.

The stress of carrying debt crosses over from your business life, to your personal life, to your marriage and family life, to your spiritual life, as well as to your personal health. All the various challenges in each of these areas become greater and more intense when you add in the debt factor.

If you are self-employed or own your own business, carrying a personal debt burden becomes a major distraction from other areas that need your undivided attention. Even if you are employed by someone else, if you are constantly worrying about debt, you are not performing your job to your fullest potential. Without looking closely into your financial history,

I can say confidently that to rise above your burden of debt, you will have to reduce and eliminate the plaguing debt. When it comes to debt, you slide into it and slowly climb back out. Benjamin Franklin is quoted as saying, "Rather to go to bed supperless than to rise in debt." Debt puts your personal living in jeopardy, and makes your spiritual discipline defenseless.

A recent survey on Monster.com asked the question, "How much does your personal debt affect the amount you earn?" Out of a total of 1,522 responses, the answers were broken down as follows:

8%	It doesn't: I can save as much of my paycheck as I want.
10%	Enough: but it doesn't hinder my savings.
40%	A lot: The amount I earn makes it hard to save.
41%	Far too much: I can barely meet my bills – never mind trying to save anything.

Recent numbers released by the Federal Reserve indicate that personal debt (credit cards, auto loans, consumer debt, etc.) exceeded $1.6 trillion. Businesses continue to write down and write off unpaid consumer debt. Bankruptcies are on the rise.

More alarming is the fact that more and more of a person's paycheck is being used to pay off debt. Wage earners are devoting an all-time high of over 15% of their take-home pay toward paying down debt. Unfortunately, the good times rarely last.

We live in a cyclical economy where ups and downs are commonplace. When the economy cools and husbands and / or wives lose their jobs, unemployment rises and debtors find themselves head over heels in debt.

What is causing the steep increase in percentages? Many professionals believe that the good times and the great economy of the past led consumers to feel they were untouchable. Nothing bad could happen to them.

Their investments seemed to be unstoppable, and their jobs secure during the good times of market bullishness and optimism, more consumers took on debt assuming that to pay it off would never be a problem. It is easy for most people to get caught up in the euphoria of good times and to overextend themselves with credit card and revolving credit-line debt.

What happens when personal debt is high and a recession overtakes the economy? Major firms lay off workers, blue collar and white collar alike. Manufacturing companies close assembly plants and unprofitable firms go out of business.

Workers remaining employed face cuts in wages and dwindling benefits. Less money in consumer pockets mean fewer goods and services are purchased. This leads to more job cuts and higher unemployment. The result becomes an even deeper recession, a continuing bad economy and an ongoing crisis.

Often this scenario presses individuals and families to purchase more things on credit, things they could not afford even before the faltering economy. They spend today's wages AND tomorrow's wages on things they think they need today.

Of course, this does not work in the long term because at some point a person simply cannot take on any more debt and has no additional cash flow to service the debt. The burden of personal debt turns difficulty into hardships and hardship into personal crisis.

To cope, individuals often pay only the monthly minimum required on revolving consumer debt. This barely covers more than the interest due, and usually takes 40 or 50 years to pay off. No, that was not a misprint you just read, it really does take that long to pay off by making minimum payments, no matter how large or how small the debt may be. Personal debt in working-class families has crippling power over their lives. It becomes a great source of anxiety and stress.

I will attempt to relate a story about crabs to carrying a heavy burden of debt. It goes like this. If you put one crab into a pot, it will climb right out. However, if you put several crabs in a pot at the same time, they will all stay there – not one will climb out. That's because as soon as one crab starts to climb out of the pot, the others grab it and drag it back down.

In a sense, debt is like a pot of crabs. When you face a personal obstacle in the area of business and try to climb out, debt pulls you down again. When you try to get out of some personal struggles and wrong habits, the burden of debt pulls at you until you start to slide backward. When trying to improve your marriage and family relationships, it seems that the stress of debt reaches out and pulls you down from your upward climb.

Debt is a heavy weight and must be eliminated. It must be expelled, driven out of your life and banished forever. It creates all kinds of debilitating pressure. It can become unbearable and weaken even the strongest person, strongest marriage, strongest business, strongest relationships and strongest financial planning. When plagued with debt that has become out of control, it is often difficult to see the whole picture of any situation, whether it be spiritual, relational or financial. Often the person carrying this kind of stress is unable to make good decisions, has clouded judgment, reacts instead of acting proactively, and seeks only short-term solutions.

Of course, all these descriptions of debt may be familiar to you. After all, that is why you purchased this book. Debt has become close to you. Although you can't exactly call it your friend, you do have an intimate relationship with it. It is on your mind every day and keeps you from enjoying the life you should be living.

It has taken over your thought life and taken control of your daily living. You have been forced to spend a great deal of time thinking about it. You devote a great deal of your paycheck to it and it keeps you from being the loving, giving person you should be.

Because of your personal debt, your life is owned by someone else or something else. Your life is not your own. You must work at that job because you need the income. You are not able to spend time in furthering your education or pursuing a career or vocation you would enjoy because you are too busy working at a job you don't like or appreciate because you need the money to pay your debt. Should you lose your present job, it would become a financial emergency in your life.

When you become debt free, for the first time perhaps, you will truly own your life. You can make money-related decisions based upon what you want and not on what others want from you. You don't have to think of the creditors first and your family second. The new situation becomes family first, all else after that.

When you become debt free, losing a job will be difficult, but not insurmountable. Yes, maybe there will be a short- term dip in your cash flow, but it won't become a financial crisis in your life. You will still be able to exist. You will still have food on the table, a roof over your head and utilities to make your living tolerable.

Break free from financial bondage. Get the right attitude! Discover how you can rise above your burden of debt!

Attitude 7

I CAN BE FINANCIALLY ACCOUNTABLE

*Y*ou can be a responsible person and you can become financially accountable for every decision you make. What is the best way to dig yourself out of a financial hole? The answer is simple – one small painful step at a time. It is easy to get into debt and difficult to climb back out of debt.

People who are in debt are usually enslaved to the advertising and marketing of our day. They have bought into the cultural attitude of "I want it, and I want it now!" Some view a pocket full of credit cards and credit lines as having financial freedom, when it really is financial bondage. Real freedom comes from being debt free.

What does accountability mean anyway? Webster's Dictionary defines accountability as "the state of being accountable, subject to the obligation to report, explain, or justify something; responsible, answerable." The Merriam-Webster's Collegiate Dictionary defines accountability as "The quality or state of being accountable; especially: an obligation or willingness to accept responsibility or to account for one's actions."

Financial accountability comes down to discipline, discipline and even more discipline. When you say "no" to credit cards and needless spending, you can then say "yes" to your financial future. Debt robs you of your dreams. Debt robs you of a vision and purpose you have for your life.

Debt can drain your strength, rob your marriage and take away of the good things that were designed for your life. Debt will crush the life out of you. This is why you must be careful to stop it before it has a death grip on your life.

One person reports that he had purchased enough merchandise to overextend his credit cards to more than $40,000. He said that by cutting every possible expense, he has reduced it by 15%. He reports that the weight of debt increases his stress and heavy burden of interest is almost unbearable. Another person notes that she has reduced her credit card debt by $15,000. Life for her now is much less stressful and she comments that she uses ONLY cash these days. She also noted that by staying focused, a rainbow is now visible just beyond the clouds.

What is the lesson to be learned here? First of all, if you don't have money, don't spend. You cannot spend money you don't have. Don't go into debt! Debt is not your friend. It is your enemy. Credit is NOT your friend. It is your enemy.

Debt sucks the life out of many marriages. Become financially responsible today, for tomorrow comes much too quickly. You don't want to be old and in debt and have little or nothing to show for it.

Debt is not fun, nor is it exciting. Being financially responsible is not some game to play. Being financially responsible is a very serious commission and should not be taken lightly. Being responsible makes you accountable. Being accountable raises questions. Anytime you are tempted to make a purchase or sign a contract, before doing so ask yourself this question: "What would happen to me if I decided to postpone this purchase for 90 days?"

If the honest answer is "nothing in particular," then don't proceed with the purchase. Because we are impulse buyers, we tend to disengage our brains before we commit to spending more money we don't have on things we do not need to impress people we really don't like. So go without all the luxuries and extras you think you may need. Most of the time you will never miss them and probably won't give it another thought.

What should you do when you are overwhelmed with debt and there seems to be no easy way out? First of all, you certainly do not want to ignore debt. Ignoring your debt problem will not make it go away. Ignoring your personal spending problem will not curb your appetite for more and more. If you need help in specific areas, seek it. Many people with problems of all kinds are ashamed and embarrassed and resist finding help. This is exactly what you should not do. Do you want to be cured? If so, swallow your pride, confess your faults and seek professional help.

Don't let anything prevent you from making the needed changes in your life. With a little help, you too can become financially accountable. Become accountable for every money decision you make each day; accountable for every purchase, every dollar and every penny. Believe me, it's worth setting aside any personal obstacle to get your life turned around.

Okay, so you have made some mistakes and have not always been financially accountable. That is unfortunate, but just remember you CAN change your behavior. It is never too late. I usually recommend paying off all debt first, assuming you have a couple of month's living expenses set aside should something happen to your job or health.

If, however, you have not yet accumulated three to six months for an emergency fund, here is another way for you to proceed. Once you have paid off one debt, take half the usual payment and add it to the payment on another debt. Take the other half of the payment and put it into a savings account. Let this accumulate each month until you have enough set aside should you experience a financial emergency. The best way to speed up this process is to get a second job and earn a second income.

What does financial accountability and responsibility feel like? How does it feel to have worked so hard and to have been successful? Try closing your eyes and getting a mind picture of a life without debt. How does it feel to be financially free? Can you feel the stress leaving your body?

All of a sudden your emotions are soaring to new highs as you see all debt disappear; no credit card debt, no car payments, no personal loans, and even no mortgage payments because your house has just been paid in full. Wow, what a great picture that is purely the result of impulse restraint. This is the result of a financially accountable person.

SETTING FINANCIAL GOALS

I would rather aim at something and miss it than to aim at nothing and hit it. Deciding to get out of debt is the first step. Think for a minute about the benefits. This action will reduce your expenses, delight your creditors, provide financial freedom and so on.

These kinds of benefits provide excellent motivation for you to set a goal of paying off all your debts. A clear goal will put you out in front of 95 people out of every 100, and you will be well on your way to becoming debt free. Just a little side comment, I've never heard of anyone getting out of debt by accident.

Determine some worthwhile financial goals. Ask this question, "Is what I want worthwhile?" Your answer to this will determine if your want is a greed or ambition. Goal setting should bring out the best in a person, allowing him or her to stretch. It should be a sacrificial achievement that is matured with time, effort and service to others. Goals that do not include service to others will eventually hinder, if not destroy, the person who has set them.

Earl Nightingale once said, "Human beings don't have trouble achieving goals: They only have trouble setting them."

In 1872, Calvin Coolidge said this, "Nothing in the world can take the place of persistence. Talent will not; nothing is more common than unsuccessful men with talent. Genius will not; unrewarded genius is almost a proverb. Education alone will not; the world is full of educated derelicts. Persistence and determination alone are omnipotent."

Orison Swett Marden says it this way, "The giants of the race have been men of concentration who have struck sledgehammer blows in one place until they have accomplished their purpose. The successful men of today are men of one overmastering idea, one unwavering aim, men of single and intense purpose."

Goals must be effective and they must be timeless in that they last through the circumstances that come in life. Financial goals that last have the following in common:

➡ Visualized

➡ Achievable

➡ Written

➡ Measurable

➡ Manageable

➡ Progress Reviewed

➡ Deadline Oriented

➡ Rewarded

What kind of financial goals are you seeking? Where are you now financially? Where would you like to see yourself? How much time do you have to reach your goals? It's not only a question of whether or not you can reach your goals, but also when you will reach those goals. Your goals and time frame play a big role in your ultimate success.

Enjoying financial security in today's world takes more than simply earning a good living. Some people who have made extraordinary incomes for many years are in terrible financial shape and are not prepared for today, let alone their future. It is essential to make decisions that will help you manage your resources if you are ever going to be financially secure.

Many Americans make enough money to become wealthy by the world's standards. The problem is not our income, but our spending. Most Americans waste much of their hard-earned money on the small things, such as a morning appointment with Starbucks for a latte and a bagel. Unfortunately, those little expenditures add up to a large outflow of our cash.

Nothing will improve your performance and your achievements more dramatically and more immediately than a clear picture of where you want to go, a plan to get there, a date of completion and a willingness to overcome obstacles in the way. Just as business and government need strong financial goals to be successful, so families also need to use a systematic approach to managing personal and household financial affairs. Your success depends upon your ability to develop personal and family financial goals and define them in a way that will ultimately achieve your objectives.

ACCOUNTABILITY WITH CLEAR GOALS

Having clear financial goals is a must. The starting point for any financial objective is first setting clear financial goals. You can accomplish just about anything if you set your mind to it and outline the necessary steps to achieve it. But it will be difficult to stay on track if you do not know where you are going. By establishing clear financial goals with specific objectives in mind, you will be well on your way to reaching the financial freedom you are looking to obtain.

We all may be created equally in the sight of God, but we usually end up very unequal. Clearly defined goals focus our vision and channel our energy. Goals are coordinates in time and space you plan to visit in the future. When you set goals, you are making an appointment with yourself to have specific things happen as a result of actions you take today.

Our lives will seldom be any better than our written goals. We make plans and we take action. You just can't hit a target you didn't aim at. Decide where you want to arrive, and begin your journey.

Goal setting works because:

➡ It focuses the mind

➡ It channels energy

➡ It gives structure to life

➡ It asks for commitment to specific accomplishments

➡ It provides motivation

➡ Reaching goals becomes habit forming

➡ Achieving results spawns new goal setting

Understanding types of financial goals first requires some personal vision. Without vision and without purpose, no financial goals can be met. Having specific financial goals is important because a lack of goals will lead to a lack of planning leading to inaction.

What is your vision for your finances? What do you want to accomplish? Where are you headed and when will you get there? Fill your thoughts with an image of what can be and what you will accomplish. Set financial goals for yourself to know just where you are going and how you will get there. Then begin to map the process.

Build a financial highway and then get started. What good is the automobile if there are no highways? What good is that power if we are only going to sit around and rev up our engines? Dreams become a reality only if you set financial goals.

Dream big, but be specific. Your financial map will tell you how to get there. By writing down and anticipating in advance the possible bends in the road ahead, your financial goals will give you direction and focus. They break down impossible undertakings into achievable tasks. They will help you keep your vision clear and your footing steady.

SHORT-TERM FINANCIAL GOALS

Short-term financial goals are things that can be accomplished in a relatively short span when compared to your lifetime goals. Maybe you are saving for a newer car, or an overseas vacation. These goals should be looked at within a 6 to 24 month period of time.

Maybe you have incurred $1,000 in debt by purchasing some new stereo equipment. You might want to get rid of this debt by breaking the goal into short little bites by saving $50 a week for the next five months. Money Magazine recently did a survey and found that 29% of Americans picked dropping debt as their number one New Year's resolution. How bad is the problem of debt in this country? Outstanding consumer debt stands at $1.7 trillion, and about 40% of it is credit card debt. Paying down debt in small amounts on a regular basis is an affordable and effective way to reach your goals. It doesn't necessarily matter how much. The key is to get into the habit of putting it away.

INTERMEDIATE FINANCIAL GOALS

Intermediate financial goals include those that can be accomplished within a one to five year horizon. This might include the purchase of a new vehicle by paying for it in cash. It might be paying off all installment debt. Another example of this might be the children's college education coming your way in five or more years. This might be the new house you have been considering or a remodeling job in your current home.

LONG-RANGE FINANCIAL GOALS

Long-range financial goals generally include things that would take you 5 to 15 or more years to accomplish. Other possibilities could be a new home or the education of a young child. This category would certainly include your retirement plans. When you set long-range financial goals, you set the stage for making sound investment decisions. Think about your goals and write them down. Then you can put together an investment opportunity aimed at reaching those desired goals.

The Hierarchy of Goals

- Daily
- Weekly
- Monthly
- Quarterly
- Annual
- Lifetime

1. The accomplishment of daily goals should lead to the achievement of weekly goals.

2. The accomplishment of weekly goals should lead to the achievement of monthly goals.

3. The accomplishment of monthly goals should lead to the achievement of quarterly goals.

4. The accomplishment of quarterly goals should lead to the achievement of annual goals.

5. The accomplishment of annual goals should lead to the achievement of lifetime goals.

MAXIMIZING YOUR FINANCIAL SUCCESS

If you would like to maximize the possibility of moving into the area of success with your business and in your personal life, consider these points.

- Accept personal responsibility for your financial success
- Allow time for relaxation
- Avoid over-commitment, watch how you spend
- Avoid problems, stay out of debt
- Be flexible to unexpected financial obstacles
- Be persistence
- Be quick to find solutions
- Change your financial plan as necessary
- Concentrate on your financial priorities
- Encourage others & yourself
- Focus on results
- Get more important things done
- Keep focused
- Know Your Passion, Purpose
- Minimize purchases that take away your focus

- Review written financial goals
- Review your budget and your progress
- Seek expert financial help
- Surround yourself with likeminded winners
- Think ahead
- When you reach one financial goal, cross it off your list and get going on the next one

Break free from financial bondage. Get the right attitude! Discover how you can be accountable!

Attitude 8

I Can Enjoy Life Without Spending Money

*M*ost of the real treasures of life can be had without spending a single penny. We all have rich resources available to us without cost.

What is the value of a great friendship or loving relationship? Everyone can extend friendship to some acquaintance. If not, endless opportunities to offer friendship can be found. How many senior citizens are living in care facilities that would love to feel the warmth of a compassionate relationship?

In the past, people lived from birth to the grave enjoying the blessings of life, yet never had to spend real money to enjoy them. Currently, we think that to enjoy life we must have money to spend.

At what monetary cost is our freedom? Our freedom of mobility, worship, independent thinking, etc., may have come at a cost to past generations, but for us we enjoy them without personal financial cost.

At what monetary cost is a walk through the forest, a rest by a rippling stream, a gaze toward a beautiful sunset, staring upward at showers of stars, a warm gentle breeze, a good read from a book of interest, a trip to the park, etc.? Equally free are enjoying the autumn colors, the white winters, the colorful spring and warm summer nights.

What about the endless puffy clouds of white that fill our sky, a glorious sunrise, and the squirrels that run from tree to tree? These are all priceless treasures of life that bring endless hours of enjoyment to us, all without costing us a dime.

Many people think that it takes money to enjoy life and all it has to offer. I am not of that crowd. Life is all about what you have inside, not what you see and accumulate on the outside. You don't need 25 years of education to take advantage of the opportunities available to you. Watch any immigrant culture and see how industrious and prosperous they can become with some hard work and simple ingenuity.

A story is told about a former prisoner of the Vietnam war. His name is Charlie. Charlie used to give speeches and presentations across the country. When he first came on the stage, he took a couple of chairs and placed them about two feet apart. As he began to talk he paced back and forth between the two chairs again and again.

Of course, the listeners were a bit puzzled, yet fascinated at the words he was speaking. They watched and listened intently. Back and forth, silently he paced. At a particular moment in his speech, Charlie then told his audience that for a period of six long years, he paced, just as he was doing now, back and forth, back and forth in his three-foot-wide North Vietnam prison cell. Then he continued his story.

It seems he was shot down by the enemy and was captured wearing only his tattered flight suit. It was all he had with him at the time of the capture. He was placed into a very tiny prison cell with only the clothes on his back. He didn't have much; or did he?

At this point in his presentation, Charlie engaged the audience, attempting to broaden their thinking and help them appreciate all they had at their disposal. He asked the listeners what else he had with him besides his flight suit. With their input, he then listed other great assets at his disposal more important than his flight suit. Some of them items on his list were as follows:

✓ his knowledge
✓ his acquired skills
✓ his training and experience
✓ his ability to think
✓ his courage
✓ his creativity
✓ his imagination

✓ his ability to reason

✓ his ability to remember

On and on the list grew until the audience suddenly began to understand that some of the best things in life are free. Some of his best assets were not the clothes on his back or the things in his possession, but rather the intangible strengths that were his.

If each of us were to do a similar exercise, we could count thousands of ways we could enjoy life without spending money.

Break free from financial bondage. Get the right attitude! Discover how you can enjoy life without spending money!

Attitude 9

I Can Find Financial Solutions

*Y*ou cannot tailor make the situations in life, but you can tailor make the attitudes to fit those situations. For many people, the income never seems to cover the outflow. This leads to arguments and high family stress. The stress often comes from deciding how much money to spend, what things to spend it on, and when to spend it.

Some of us spend more time reacting to the fact that we have a problem than we do solving the problem – problems are inevitable. Some problems can be anticipated. Some are surprises. The idea that problems occur regularly need never be a surprise.

The good news is that for every problem, there's a solution. Sometimes the solution is immediate. Sometimes, it takes awhile to discover. Sometimes, the solution involves letting go. When you leave your financial problems unsolved, you in essence are leaving them to chance. You need a plan, a budget and action steps or your financial problems will never go away.

Sometimes problems are a warning sign that you are on the wrong track. You can learn to identify which problems are trying to lead you in a new direction and which ones simply ask to be solved.

All of us have definite ideas about how we are doing financially and just what we want our money to do for us. All of us must take those ideas and commit them to a plan, a financial road map, if you will. This financial plan becomes the written answer, the on paper solution to our financial challenges. You can learn to focus on the solution rather than on the problem and maintain a positive attitude toward life. Things work out best for those who make the best of the way things work out.

What kind of financial solutions do you need to find in your life? Do you have excessive debt? Are you facing college bills for yourself or your children? Are you single, but need to save for marriage? Are you planning to purchase a house or are you simply facing the financial challenge of preparing for your long-term future?

The way to connect all these dots is through the design of a good financial plan. This plan, like a good road map, shows you exactly your current financial picture, where you are now, where you wish to be in the future, and what steps to take to get you there. It answers the standard questions of how, what, why, when and where.

What is your solution? What is your plan? Let me suggest an uncomplicated beginning plan that sounds so simplistic that it just might work for you. You can condense it all down to just five words. That is: spend less and save more.

Spending less is a simple answer, but it's not so easy to accomplish. Perhaps you have formed bad money management habits that have haunted you for years. Don't you think now would be a good time break the bands of bondage? You can spend less by eliminating wasteful spending.

Do you really need those expensive toys you only use a few times a year? Sometimes the maintenance and insurance alone for SUVs, motorcycles, boats, RVs, guns, wave runners, snowmobiles and other cash-draining hobbies can run into the hundreds, if not thousands of dollars (this amount, of course, is after the initial purchase cost).

Saving more is the financial solution. Of course you cannot save until you eliminate the debt and payments to service your debt. That frees up cash to save more. If you are a consumer with bad spending habits, you are probably adding to your debt load every month. If so, now is the time to rein in your spending and change those bad habits. Change those bad-spending habits into good-savings habits.

When you find solutions to your financial problems, your personal stress level goes way down. When you waste less money, you have more cash to pay down debt. Paying down debt frees your cash to be saved and invested.

Your hard-earned dollars won't be spent on frivolous purchases. This means your long hours and work-filled weeks will be used to make your retirement years more comfortable instead of your current days and weeks more stressful.

FINDING FINANCIAL SOLUTIONS

Financial solutions come about with advance planned money management, as opposed to crisis money management. Setting financial goals in advance of all income and expenses *give you control.* As is the case with most successful people, you've probably focused more on making money than bothering with learning how to manage it. Although you have your attorney, your insurance agent, your banker, your CPA and your broker, you may not have given a lot of thought to a sound financial plan.

Have you strategized in a way that will enable you to reach your financial goals? You need to. Your financial well being and success will not come by sheer luck and inattention to your goals. In fact, that will guarantee your family economic disaster. Financial goals are reached by knowing what you want, where you are going, making informed choices and using all appropriated strategies to set out on your course.

Setting financial goals *takes the control from others and puts the control of your financial future into your hands.* It becomes your blueprint that will guide you through the financial peaks and valleys of life.

Without spending limits and preparations for your financial future by setting current goals, you, your dependents and your assets are not adequately protected against the risks of life. This can lead to needless waste of your current resources. Your daily decision making could be controlled by your current desires, not your future needs. If you do not take control of your financial possessions now, you will likely pay higher income taxes, which may have been avoided with a sound financial plan.

Setting financial goals *points you in the right direction.* It helps point you toward specific family goals and gives you leverage over your financial resources.

What do you need your resources to do for you? Without setting proper financial goals, your long-term needs will not be met. Your children won't have a means to get a good education, your spouse will not be prepared in case of your disability or death and you will be forced to live on a retirement income of much less than you might need.

Setting financial goals *helps you know yourself.* Financial success begins by knowing yourself. This includes knowing your objectives, determining your investment goals, your lifestyle and the type of investment goals that make you comfortable.

Because your goals and needs are unique to you, making wise investment choices is very important. You will learn about yourself by taking into account your investment objectives, your tolerance for risk, your time horizon, your financial knowledge and your financial health. Another part of knowing yourself is setting realistic expectations. Are you one who can accept higher risk for higher potential returns?

Conversely, will you be satisfied with lower returns by choosing conservative investments? The best way to get to know yourself, and to start down the path to achieving your financial goals, is to get time on your side. This can only be maximized if you begin at once.

Setting financial goals *keeps you on track.* Living in a busy world with all sorts of demands and opportunities to spend can play havoc with our available financial resources. We all have some sort of money challenges from time to time. It's part of life and living. This is why setting financial goals are so important. How can you possibly think about the future that is 10, 20 and 30 years away, when your checkbook is now empty and you won't get paid for another 10 days!

Setting financial goals *helps you make the appropriate decisions* based upon your previously written goals, when attempts are made to rob you of your cash. Your money will actually seem to go further if you know where it goes. Know what you want to accomplish with your income, know what is wise spending and where you are spending foolishly and carefully plan your spending in advance.

Taking the time to carefully plan for your financial future is the act of accepting personal responsibility for it. Certainly, there will be times when you need information and advice from outside sources, but the ultimate decisions are yours. By staying on track with your financial goals, you will increase your ability to get what you want out of life.

Setting financial goals *helps you to build financial assets*. Whatever your choice of an investment vehicle, without a goal, you are likely just to hit and miss. Your last choice for spending available income is going to be putting it away for your retirement. This means that whatever is left at the end of the week is what you will save.

Your savings will not grow unless you make it your first choice of what to do with each paycheck. A definite spending goal will help you build assets. You can begin to build assets by first limiting the taxes you are currently paying. The goal of every taxpayer should be to pay your fair share and to pay everything that is legally owed. Tax evasion is both illegal and immoral. Tax avoidance through proper planning, however, is both legal and moral.

Setting financial goals *helps you prepare for retirement*. Many uncertainties surround the subject of retirement. These include the uncertainty of your health, the economy, inflation, your age, the success of your investments and more. Because of this, it is of vital importance that you start when you are young before time becomes your enemy. And even if you are ready to retire, setting financial goals is still important.

We are living longer than ever before and the uncertainty of inflation and other expenses should cause us to commit to careful planning and strategic goals. When investing, it is important to take a long-term view, giving your investments time to grow.

Setting financial goals *helps with educational expenses*. In building your overall family asset base, discuss with your family what goals they might have in mind. Of course, for the parents, this includes retirement plans. For the children, it definitely includes their education.

One of the greatest gifts parents can give their children is a good education. Instead of funneling large sums of money for furniture or a vehicle, let them earn their own money, but give them a head start in their earning potential by helping them get a solid education. This will cut their umbilical cord to your purse strings, enabling them to gain earning power themselves.

Every family must spend according to its family values. This is how to set financial goals. It is not that values are right or wrong, rather that values vary from family to family. The purchase of a new house or maybe a new business start–up could be planned in your future, as well as an infinite list of other possibilities. Building assets for additional, yet unknown, projects also requires that you continue to set and consider future financial goals, and now is the time to begin.

Setting financial goals *prepares you for the unexpected.* One general goal is to help you protect yourself against a number of risks. These might include the loss of income, the death of a family member, medical expenses, disability, unemployment, property and liability losses, and others. At the very least, goals help you set up an emergency fund to act as a buffer for unplanned expenses.

Change is a way of life. Things happen. Life isn't always smooth. Jobs are lost. Health problems confront. Vehicles break down. Emergencies arise. Most experts recommend setting aside anywhere from six months' to a year's salary in liquid assets, such as CDs or money market accounts. In addition, it is important to purchase disability income, life, long-term care, or other types of insurance to help protect you, your family and your assets against the loss of income, illness, disability or other financial circumstances.

When you recognize the possibility of mishaps that will affect your finances, you can plan for their occurrence in advance. You may have to make slight changes or adjustments in your financial goals, but should something unforeseen come your way, the financial burden can be lessened. Your advance planning can lessen your anxiety and reduce the effect of a potentially severe blow to your finances.

Setting financial goals improves communication within families. Setting financial goals, launching those goals and staying on track is a family team effort. Setting goals is full of tough choices. People who do not have a lot of extra income will have to prioritize their spending and separate their needs from their wants and desires. They may not get the house of their dreams, a new car every couple of years or the education for their children at the best private colleges available. Families have to be willing to accept trade-offs.

If you have a family, you all must come together to build a sure financial base. If one family member controls spending and promotes saving and the others do not, you will only reach a small portion of the assets you are attempting to build. Each family member should contribute to setting the goals, determining the priorities and considering the various consequences of abandoning the goals. By working together, it becomes a family project that enhances unity, stable relationships and a method to keep each family member on track.

To be successful at anything necessitates knowledge of goal setting, measuring progress and achieving milestones. In its simplest form, goal setting includes the following steps.

WRITE DOWN YOUR FINANCIAL GOALS

Use paper and pen, or your computer, to crystallize your thinking. Writing down your goals leads to commitment. You become open to new ideas about what you really want to accomplish. This helps you prepare and ready yourself for the future.

Writing down your ideas makes you available to new opportunities. Gather all of the information you have relating to your current financial condition, your assessment of where you are and where you want to be, and begin to gather all the necessary paperwork.

You will need to know exactly where your income is coming from and what your spending habits are. Be very detailed. You must know about your employee benefits, insurance benefits, any insurance policies you have purchased, your living will, a complete and detailed statement of your net worth, a personal income and expense statement, the likely cost of your child's future education, your retirement desires, and in short, a written document of your past, present and future financial situation.

This will take some time, but you cannot prepare written financial goals without some intimate knowledge of your financial situation. Have you analyzed your history of spending? Have you examined your spending habits? Have you investigated all future costs? Do you know the source of your financial leaks? Have you found the holes in your budget, and identified areas requiring immediate change?

Know your purpose, your objectives and your specific goals. If your objective is to be financially sound, what specific goals will you set for your future to obtain? Define clearly what those goals are. Where are you going? Where do you want to be? How will you get there? Which goals are for next month, and which ones are for five years from now? What are your priorities?

GIVE YOURSELF A DEADLINE

Specify a time for achieving your objective. Get started on your financial journey by being deadline motivated. Deadlines help get you started and keep you moving. You become a person on a mission. You have a target. Goals are worthless without a plan of action and some deadlines. Develop specific deadlines that will keep you on track toward meeting that goal.

In the beginning you will need to set up a budget. Consider having automatic payroll deductions for savings or retirement purposes, a plan for contributing to your employer's 401(k) program, contributing to your own IRA account, and so on. Look at those specific deadlines, prioritize them and then put them into action.

Financial goals and objectives should cover all time elements. They should anticipate changing needs as your life changes. It is never too early to understand your purpose, organize those objectives in a clear, concise manner, and then set the appropriate goals that will put you on your path to financial freedom.

SET YOUR STANDARDS HIGH

In general, the higher you set your goal, the more effort you will have to expend toward reaching it. The more lofty the goal, the more motivated you will be to reach it. As you reach certain milestones in your blueprint of progress, you'll become inspired to give it all you've got to reach your desired result. It is a strange thing that often it takes just as much effort, energy and hard work to reach small goals, that lead to little more than poverty and misery, as it does to reach higher goals that lead to success, prosperity and abundance. So aim high! If you shoot for the moon and miss it, at least you'll still be among the stars.

SET REALISTIC, OBTAINABLE GOALS

Be levelheaded and pragmatic when setting your financial goals. Goals that are set too high, so that they become unattainable, will be a source of never-ending frustration for you and possibly your family. While they might look very good on paper, if you cannot reach them, you may eventually abandon all your goals and simply give up.

BE DETAILED AND SPECIFIC

Explicit objectives and precise family financial goals must be set. Goals that are vague might never be met. Don't ballpark your numbers or your goals. Don't say to your family, "Let's buy a small farm in the valley in a few years." Or to your spouse, "Let's set a goal of moving to Mexico when we retire." Though serving in a Third World country might be your purpose, and retiring in Mexico might be your objective, when it comes to setting goals, the numbers must be very clear. Numbers include your age, the year, the dollars needed, and every other detail that might enter into this picture.

BE FLEXIBLE

Each of your goals must be accommodating to whatever life brings your way. Situations change, people change, desires and wants all change family goals. Be prepared to be elastic with whatever state your family affairs changes your course. Every pilot expects that "course corrections" (changes in wind direction and velocity, inclement weather, payload, etc.) will be necessary during flight. If you have a family to consider, within the family unit, changes that affect goals and plans might include health, family size or income.

BEGIN WITH THE FIRST STEP

Start now–right now. Ask questions, do research and consult a professional. Get the advice and information you need to create a plan today. It is important to think it all through. It's important to blueprint your strategic plan. It's also important to see the eventual result.

One does not always know all the forks in the road when beginning the journey. But if you know where you are now and where you want to be, then you can start with what you know and get moving to where you want to be. You probably already have some ideas about just what kind of goals would be of interest to you or your family members. Setting goals gives you a direction.

The best way to get started is to just start! Don't get caught up in the little things and miss the big picture! By never getting started, you are being defeated by time. If you move ahead and do not get bogged down with the daily problems and challenges of life, you can make time your friend. Time is either your greatest asset or your worst enemy.

Break free from financial bondage. Get the right attitude! Discover how you can find financial solutions!

Attitude 10

I Can Change My Attitude – I Can Change My Life

*a*TTITUDE isn't simply a state of mind; it is also a reflection of what we value. Attitude is more than just saying we can; it is believing we can.

Attitude requires believing before seeing, because seeing is based on circumstances, believing is based on faith. Attitude is contagious, especially when we ready ourselves for our tomorrows.

We have total ownership of our attitudes. No one else has the power to alter our attitudes without our permission. Our attitude allows us to become more empowering than money, to rise above our failures, and accept others for who they are, and what they say.

Attitude is more important than giftedness, and is the forerunner of all skills needed for happiness and success. Our attitudes can be used to build us up or put us down – the choice is ours.

Attitude also gives us the wisdom to know that we can't change events of the past. I am convinced that life is 10% what happens to me, and 90% how I respond to it – and with this state of mind, I remain in charge of my attitude.

Billy Graham said, "If a person gets his attitude towards money straight, it will help straighten out almost every other area of his life. Tell me what you think about money, and I can tell you what you think about God, for these two are closely related. A man's heart is closer to his wallet than almost anything else."

Attitude is a choice! We have the power to choose our responses to any situation. Two kinds of choice-point filters have a profound impact on our responses; those within and those outside of our control.

Some choice influences, such as gender and age, are outside our control. Others, such as values and education, are within our control. Through our attitude, we can empower the elements within our control while minimizing the effect of those outside our control.

Outside Our Control	Within Our Control
Race	Feelings
Sex	Thoughts
Age	Attitudes
Country of Origin	Values
Birth Family	Desires
Physical Attributes	Education
Other Choices	My Choices

Whether within or outside our control, our attitude can greatly influence our response to the circumstances of life. Do financial setbacks come our way? Of course. Do they have to keep us down? Certainly not!

The attitudes and habits we cultivate, measure the harvest we reap in our lives. Blessed people can be found everywhere. Successful businesspersons are everywhere. They are not extraordinary people, although many have lived extraordinary lives. All have particular qualities in common. These are not qualities you inherit, rather you must develop them through education and through hard work. It's not what happens to you that counts as much as how you react to what happens.

Your attitude is one of the few things in life you can control. Although you can't foresee the ups and downs you'll experience, you can control how you'll react to them.

THE BUCKETS

I read a little story about two little buckets who were on their way to the well. These were talking buckets!

"You look mighty sad," said one bucket to the other.

"I was just thinking about the uselessness of what we do," said the sad bucket. "Time after time we go down to the well and get full, but we always come back to the well empty."

"You've got the wrong slant," said the other bucket. "I enjoy what we're doing. The way I look at it, no matter how many times we come to the well empty, we always leave full."

Attitudes are highly contagious. They can have a profound effect on the people with whom we live and work. Choose to be a positive person!

ATTRIBUTES OF SUCCESS

➡ **Determination**: Be persistent, especially when you fail

➡ **Honesty**: Always speak and live the truth

➡ **Responsibility**: Be trustworthy and dependable

➡ **Thoughtfulness**: Think of others before yourself

➡ **Confidentiality**: Don't share information you know to be confidential or that you have been asked to keep to yourself.

➡ **Punctuality**: Be on time, every time

➡ **Self-control**: Make wise decisions. Don't let emotion lead you astray or let a fear of being wrong hold you back from making decisions

➡ **Patience:**Whether you're eager to speak next or to reach your next goal, accept that "your turn will come." This doesn't mean settling for inaction, however. Being patient isn't the same as being complacent

➡ **Purity**: Reject anything that lowers your personal standards or the standards of those you serve

➡ **Compassion**: To offer compassion is always one of life's rich experiences.

PRACTICES OF SUCCESS

- Involve others in developing "common visions."
- Express your viewpoint, but be open to what others think.
- Set clear objectives and milestones to check your progress toward your goals.
- Focus on excellence, not perfection.
- Encourage others to express their ideas.
- Create a trusting environment that encourages learning.
- Focus on team building and address issues that build barriers to effective group communication.

OPTIMISTS AND PESSIMISTS

Have you heard this story? What does the optimist say about the glass and the water? (It's half full!) And what does the pessimist say? (It's half empty!) Finally what does the process reengineer say about it? ("It looks like you've got twice as much glass as you need there.")

All of us have the freedom to make choices in life. No one tells us which choices to make; we have complete freedom to make our choices. Attitude is a choice. Don't choose negativity. Choose to be an optimist – to believe in yourself and others. Associate with positive leaders.

Seek advice from those who are firmly in control of their finances. Get advice from those who have become debt free. If they have become successful in this area of their personal lives, then you can, too!

Watch your financial attitude! Are you seeking a solution or just looking for more problems? Do you tend to see the dark side of things or the bright side of things? Are you trying to be an optimist or a pessimist?

"People inhabit this earth by the billions. Flocks increase, plants grow. When I was younger there was much talk about a population explosion and prediction of famine, or scarcity. Food was to run out, the life as we know it was to end. But things kept getting better. Technology lets fewer farmers produce more food. New discoveries of oil and gas occur. Whole industries which did not exist in the 50s and 60s now employ millions. There simply is no credible law of scarcity. We have abundance in this earth. Computer chips from sand, service industries, information and processing ideas, as in the communication arena. It is the opposite of the predictions." Wade B. Cook in Business Buy The Bible

DEFEATING ATTITUDE

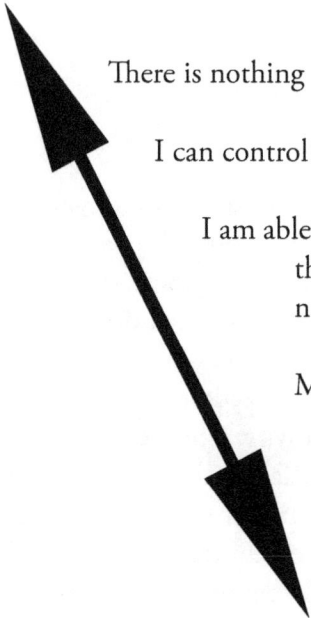

There is nothing in my life that I can influence.

I can control a few things in my environment

I am able to control several things in my life, but there are many things over which I do not have any control.

Most of my environment is controllable.

I am capable of influencing everything that life deals to me.

WINNING ATTITUDE

THE FARMERS

Here is a very old, but humorous, story: There were two farmers. One was a pessimist, the other was an optimist. The optimist would say, "What a beautiful day, lots of sunshine." The pessimist would respond, "Yes, but I'm afraid too much sunshine will scorch the crops." The optimist would say, "We had such a nice rainfall." The pessimist would respond, "Yes, but I'm afraid too much rain will flood the crops."

One day the optimist said to the pessimist. "Have you seen my new bird dog? He is the finest dog money can buy!" The pessimist answered and said, "You mean that mutt I saw penned up behind your house? He didn't look like much to me!"

The optimist said to the pessimist, "How about going hunting with me tomorrow?" The pessimist agreed to go. The two farmers went on a hunting trip. They shot some ducks. The optimist ordered his dog to get the ducks.

The dog obediently responded. But instead of swimming in the water after the ducks, the dog walked on top of the water, retrieved the ducks, and then walked back to his owner still walking on top of the water.

The optimist turned to the pessimist and said, "Now, just what do you think of my dog?" After pondering the question, the pessimist replied, "Hmmm, your dog can't swim, can he?"

Aren't we all like that at times? We can't see the good in our financial world because we focus on faults or problems. Someone once said, "In the middle of every difficulty lies opportunity."

The Bible speaks about focusing on the right things.
Philippians 4:8

> *"Finally, brothers, whatever is true, whatever is noble, whatever is right, whatever is pure, whatever is lovely, whatever is admirable – if anything is excellent or praiseworthy – think about such things".*

A winning attitude helps you to:

- Break out of your box that restricts inspiration, and limits your potential
- Break Your Bad Habits
- View Failures As Opportunities
- Think In Positives And Potential
- Try Out New Ways And Ideas
- Breakdown Barriers To Creativity
- Embrace New Perspectives
- Forget your traditional perspective and approach change from other viewpoints.

PRACTICE CREATIVITY

Try new ideas, new solutions to problems, new ways of doing things, etc.

> "While it is possible for people with great talent or drive to achieve with a bad attitude, it doesn't happen very often, and it takes an incredible amount of effort. And even if they do achieve some degree of success, they aren't happy. Most often, people with bad attitudes don't get very far in life." John C. Maxwell in *Today Matters*

Attitude is more than just saying "I can"; it's believing you can. It requires believing before seeing, because seeing is based on circumstances, believing is based on faith.

Success is an attitude and our attitude makes all the difference in a productive and successful financial life.

Break free from financial bondage. Get the right attitude! Discover how you can change your attitude and change your life!

SUMMARY

*N*othing will improve your performance and your achievements more dramatically and more immediately than a clear picture of where you want to go, a plan to get there, a date of completion and a willingness to overcome obstacles in the way. Just as business and government need strong financial goals to be successful, so each of us also need to use a systematic approach to managing personal and household financial affairs.

But it is next to impossible to achieve any financial goals if your attitude is flawed. Flawed attitudes prohibit success even if your objectives and goals are honorable. Take one more look at the 10 attitudes of financial success.

Attitude 1: I Can Be Debt Free

Attitude 2: I Can Break Bad Spending Habits

Attitude 3: I Can Choose to Pay Cash

Attitude 4: I Can Renew My Thinking

Attitude 5: I Can Change My Flawed Value System

Attitude 6: I Can Rise Above My Burden of Debt

Attitude 7: I Can Be Financially Accountable

Attitude 8: I Can Enjoy Life Without Spending Money

Attitude 9: I Can Find Financial Solutions

Attitude 10: I Can Change My Attitude – I Can Change My Life

Your financial success depends upon your ability to develop good personal attitudes toward the management and investment of your income and assets. Change your attitude…change your life!

Source Material

21 Unbreakable Laws of Success, Max Anders, Thomas Nelson, 1996

A Christian Guide to Prosperity; Fries & Taylor, California: Communications Research, 1984

A Look At Stewardship, Word Aflame Publications, 2001

American Savings Education Council (http://www.asec.org)

Anointed For Business, Ed Silvoso, Regal, 2002

Avoiding Common Financial Mistakes, Ron Blue, Navpress, 1991

Baker Encyclopedia of the Bible; Walter Elwell, Michigan: Baker Book House, 1988

Becoming The Best, Barry Popplewell, England: Gower Publishing Company Limited, 1988

Business Proverbs, Steve Marr, Fleming H. Revell, 2001

Cheapskate Monthly, Mary Hunt

Commentary on the Old Testament; Keil-Delitzsch, Michigan: Eerdmans Publishing, 1986

Crown Financial Ministries, various publications

Customers As Partners, Chip Bell, Texas: Berrett-Koehler Publishers, 1994

Cut Your Bills in Half; Pennsylvania: Rodale Press, Inc., 1989

Debt-Free Living, Larry Burkett, Dimensions, 2001

Die Broke, Stephen M. Pollan & Mark Levine, HarperBusiness, 1997

Double Your Profits, Bob Fifer, Virginia: Lincoln Hall Press, 1993

Eerdmans' Handbook to the Bible, Michigan: William B. Eerdmans Publishing Company, 1987

Eight Steps to Seven Figures, Charles B. Carlson, Double Day, 2000

Everyday Life in Bible Times; Washington DC: National Geographic Society, 1967

Financial Dominion, Norvel Hayes, Harrison House, 1986

Financial Freedom, Larry Burkett, Moody Press, 1991

Financial Freedom, Patrick Clements, VMI Publishers, 2003

Financial Peace, Dave Ramsey, Viking Press, 2003

Financial Self-Defense; Charles Givens, New York: Simon And Schuster, 1990

Flood Stage, Oral Roberts, 1981

Generous Living, Ron Blue, Zondervan, 1997

Get It All Done, Tony and Robbie Fanning, New York:Pennsylvania: Chilton Book, 1979

Getting Out of Debt, Howard Dayton, Tyndale House, 1986

Getting Out of Debt, Mary Stephenson, Fact Sheet 436, University of Maryland Cooperative Extension Service, 1988

Giving and Tithing, Larry Burkett, Moody Press, 1991

God's Plan For Giving, John MacArthur, Jr., Moody Press, 1985

God's Will is Prosperity, Gloria Copeland, Harrison House, 1978

Great People of the Bible and How They Lived; New York: Reader's Digest, 1974

How Others Can Help You Get Out of Debt; Esther M. Maddux, Circular 759-3,

How To Make A Business Plan That Works, Henderson, North Island Sound Limited, 1989

How To Manage Your Money, Larry Burkett, Moody Press, 1999

How to Personally Profit From the Laws of Success, Sterling Sill, NIFP, Inc., 1978

How to Plan for Your Retirement; New York: Corrigan & Kaufman, Longmeadow Press, 1985

Is God Your Source?, Oral Roberts, 1992

It's Not Luck, Eliyahu Goldratt, Great Barrington, MA: The North River Press, 1994

Jesus CEO, Laurie Beth Jones, Hyperion, 1995

John Avanzini Answers Your Questions About Biblical Economics, Harrison House, 1992

Living on Less and Liking It More, Maxine Hancock, Chicago, Illinois: Moody Press, 1976

Making It Happen; Charles Conn, New Jersey: Fleming H. Revell Company, 1981

Master Your Money Or It Will Master You, Arlo E. Moehlenpah, Doing Good Ministries, 1999

Master Your Money; Ron Blue, Tennessee: Thomas Nelson, Inc. 1986

Miracle of Seed Faith, Oral Roberts, 1970

Mississippi State University Extension Service

Money, Possessions, and Eternity, Randy Alcorn, Tyndale House, 2003

More Than Enough, David Ramsey, Penguin Putnam Inc, 2002

Moving the Hand of God, John Avanzini, Harrison House, 1990

Multiplication, Tommy Barnett, Creation House, 1997

NebFacts, Nebraska Cooperative Extension

New York Post

One Up On Wall Street; New York: Peter Lynch, Simon And Schuster, 1989

Personal Finances, Larry Burkett, Moody Press, 1991

Portable MBA in Finance and Accounting; Livingstone, Canada: John Wiley & Sons, Inc., 1992

Principle-Centered Leadership, Stephen R. Covey, New York: Summit Books, 1991

Principles of Financial Management, Kolb & DeMong, Texas: Business Publications, Inc., 1988

Rapid Debt Reduction Strategies, John Avanzini, HIS Publishing, 1990

Real Wealth, Wade Cook, Arizona: Regency Books, 1985

See You At The Top, Zig Ziglar, Louisianna: Pelican Publishing Company, 1977

Seed-Faith Commentary on the Holy Bible, Oral Roberts, Pinoak Publications, 1975

Sharkproof, Harvey Mackay, New York: HarperCollins Publishers, 1993

Smart Money, Ken and Daria Dolan, New York: Random House, Inc., 1988

Strong's Concordance, Tennessee: Crusade Bible Publishers, Inc.,

Success by Design, Peter Hirsch, Bethany House, 2002

Success is the Quality of your Journey, Jennifer James, New York: Newmarket Press, 1983

Swim with the Sharks Without Being Eaten Alive, Harvey Mackay, William Morrow , 1988

The Almighty and the Dollar; Jim McKeever, Oregon: Omega Publications, 1981

The Challenge, Robert Allen, New York: Simon And Schuster, 1987

The Family Financial Workbook, Larry Burkett, Moody Press, 2002

The Management Methods of Jesus, Bob Briner, Thomas Nelson, 1996

The Millionaire Next Door, Thomas Stanley & William Danko, Pocket Books, 1996

The Money Book for Kids, Nancy Burgeson, Troll Associates,1992

The Money Book for King's Kids; Harold E. Hill, New Jersey: Fleming H. Revell Company, 1984

The Seven Habits of Highly Effective People, Stephen Covey, New York: Simon And Schuster, 1989

The Wealthy Barber, David Chilton, California: Prima Publishing, 1991

Theological Wordbook of the Old Testament, Chicago, Illinois: Moody Press, 1981

Treasury of Courage and Confidence, Norman Vincent Peale, New York: Doubleday & Co., 1970

True Prosperity, Dick Iverson, Bible Temple Publishing, 1993

Trust God For Your Finances, Jack Hartman, Lamplight Publications, 1983

University of Georgia Cooperative Extension Service, 1985

Virginia Cooperative Extension

Webster's Unabridged Dictionary, Dorset & Baber, 1983

What Is an Entrepreneur; David Robinson, MA: Kogan Page Limited, 1990

Word Meanings in the New Testament, Ralph Earle, Michigan: Baker Book House, 1986

Word Pictures in the New Testament; Robertson, Michigan: Baker Book House, 1930

Word Studies in the New Testament; Vincent, New York: Charles Scribner's Sons, 1914

Worth

You Can Be Financially Free, George Fooshee, Jr., 1976, Fleming H. Revell Company.

Your Key to God's Bank, Rex Humbard, 1977

Your Money Counts, Howard, Dayton, Tyndale House, 1997

Your Money Management, MaryAnn Paynter, Circular 1271, University of Illinois Cooperative Extension Service, 1987.

Your Money Matters, Malcolm MacGregor, Bethany Fellowship, Inc., 1977

Your Road to Recovery, Oral Roberts, Oliver Nelson, 1986

COMMENTS ON SOURCES

Over the years I have collected bits and pieces of interesting material, written notes on sermons I've heard, jotted down comments on financial articles I've read, and gathered a lot of great information. It is unfortunate that I didn't record the sources of all of these notes in my earlier years. I gratefully extend my appreciation to the many writers, authors, teachers and pastors from whose articles and sermons I have gleaned much insight.

Rich Brott

ONLINE RESOURCES

American Savings Education Council (http://www.asec.org)

Bloomberg.com (http://www.bloomberg.com)

Bureau of the Public Debt Online (http://www.publicdebt.treas.gov)

BusinessWeek (http://www.businessweek.com)

Charles Schwab & Co., Inc. (http://www.schwab.com)

Consumer Federation of America (http://www.consumerfed.org)

Debt Advice.org (http://www.debtadvice.org)

Federal Reserve System (http://www.federalreserve.gov)

Fidelity Investments (http://www.fidelity.com)

Financial Planning Association (http://www.fpanet.org)

Forbes (www.forbes.com)

Fortune Magazine (http://www.fortune.com)

Generous Giving (http://www.generousgiving.org/)

Investing for Your Future (http://www.investing.rutgers.edu)

Kiplinger Magazine (http://www.kiplinger.com/)

Money Magazine (http://money.cnn.com)

MorningStar (http://www.morningstar.com)

MSN Money (http://moneycentral.msn.com)

Muriel Siebert (http://www.siebertnet.com)

National Center on Education and the Economy (http://www.ncee.org)

National Foundation for Credit Counseling (http://www.nfcc.org)

Quicken (http://www.quicken.com)

Smart Money (http://www.smartmoney.com)

Social Security Online (http://www.ssa.gov)

Standard & Poor's (http://www2.standardandpoors.com)

The Dollar Stretcher, Gary Foreman, (http://www.stretcher.com)

The Vanguard Group (http://flagship.vanguard.com)

U.S. Securities and Exchange Commission (http://www.sec.gov)

Yahoo! Finance (http://finance.yahoo.com)

Magazine Resources

Business Week
Consumer Reports
Forbes
Kiplinger's Personal Finance
Money
Smart Money
US News and World Report

NEWSPAPER RESOURCES

Barrons
Investors Business Daily
USA Today
Wall Street Journal
Washington Times

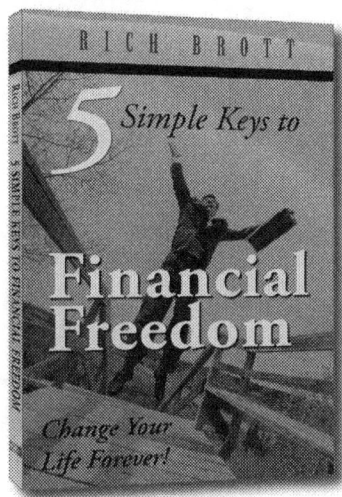

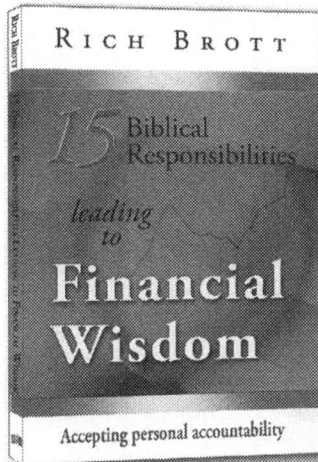

Additional Resources by Rich Brott

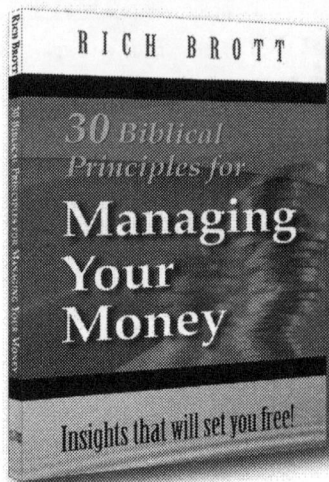

30 Biblical Principles for Managing Your Money

Insights that Will Set You Free!

By Rich Brott

6" x 9", 160 pages
ISBN 1-60185-012-3
ISBN (EAN) 978-1-60185-012-6

a b c
Book Publishing

www.AbcBookPublishing.com

Additional Resources by Rich Brott

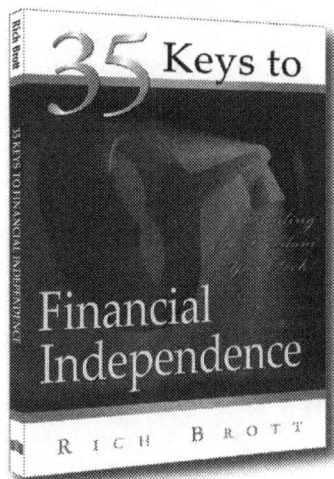

35 Keys to
Financial Independence

Finding the Freedom You Seek!

By Rich Brott

6" x 9", 176 pages
ISBN 1-60185-020-4
ISBN (EAN) 978-1-60185-020-1

abc
Book Publishing

Order online at:

www.amazon.com
www.barnesandnoble.com
www.booksamillion.com
www.citychristianpublishing.com
www.walmart.com

www.AbcBookPublishing.com

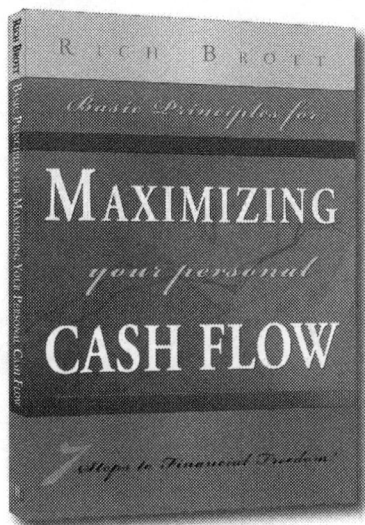

Additional Resources by Rich Brott

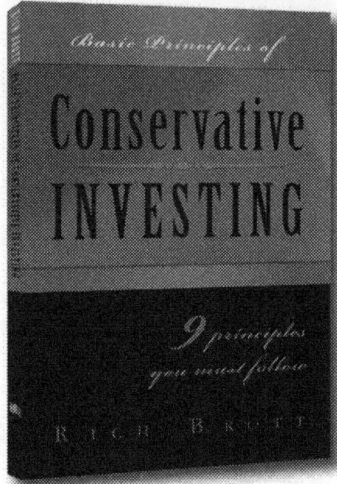

Basic Principles of Conservative Investing

9 Principles You Must Follow

By Rich Brott

6" x 9", 116 pages
ISBN 1-60185-018-2
ISBN (EAN) 978-1-60185-018-8

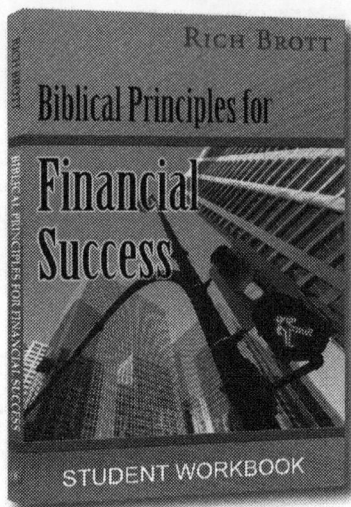

Biblical Principles for Financial Success

Student Workbook

By Rich Brott

7.5" x 9.25", 228 pages
ISBN 1-60185-016-6
ISBN (EAN) 978-1-60185-016-4

abc
Book Publishing

Order online at:

www.amazon.com
www.barnesandnoble.com
www.booksamillion.com
www.citychristianpublishing.com
www.walmart.com

www.AbcBookPublishing.com

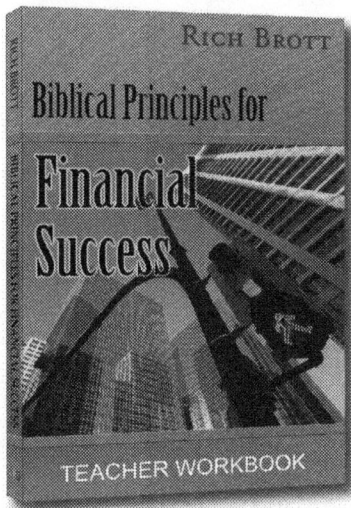

Additional Resources by Rich Brott

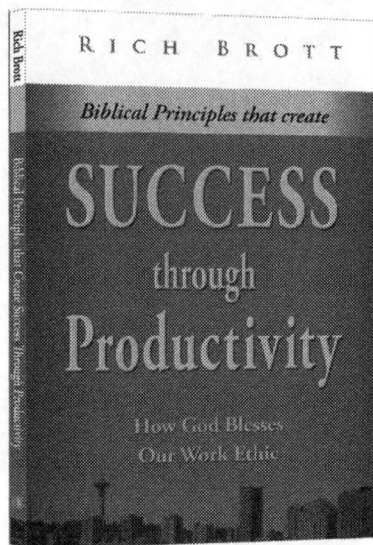

Biblical Principles that Create Success through Productivity

How God Blesses Our Work Ethic

By Rich Brott

6" x 9", 224 pages
ISBN 1-60185-007-7
ISBN (EAN) 978-1-60185-007-2

abc
Book Publishing

www.AbcBookPublishing.com